RiO

The Power of Coincidence

THE POWER OF COINCIDENCE

How Life Shows Us What We Need to Know

DAVID RICHO

Shambhala
Boston & London
2007

Shambhala Publications, Inc.
Horticultural Hall
300 Massachusetts Avenue
Boston, Massachusetts 02115
www.shambhala.com

9 8 7 6 5 4 3 2 1

Printed in the United States of America

⊗ This edition is printed on acid-free paper that meets the American National Standards Institute z39.48 Standard. Distributed in the United States by Random House, Inc., and in Canada by Random House of Canada Ltd

Designed by Jeff Baker

Library of Congress Cataloging-in-Publication Data
Richo, David, 1940–
The power of coincidence: how life shows us what we need to know/David Richo.
   p. cm.
ISBN 978-1-59030-427-3 (alk. paper)
   1. Coincidence. I. Title.
BF1175.R535 2007
123—dc22
2006035785

To Josh, my son, a synchronicity of love and joy:
Already by age eight, nature had taught you
    the deepest human paradox:
Running so elatedly to the edge of the pond,
with the bread you had carefully broken—
duck-bite-size—
your face, alight with impassioned expectation,
fell
in disappointment and despair:
not one white feather anywhere.
The choice: keep your bread
or cast it upon the waters anyway:
tardy ducks might come
some other—Joshless—day.
A toss—
and suddenly, O your surprised eyes,
your revived face!
An arrow of ducks
came gliding, single-pointedly, to your feet:
more than ever you had expected,
coming closer than ever you had hoped,
from thin air, from nowhere, from everywhere.

May it always happen like that, Josh.

Contents

CONTENTS

Preface

This book was originally published more than a decade ago under the title *Unexpected Miracles: The Gift of Synchronicity and How to Open It.* Since that time, my understanding of meaningful coincidence has deepened in many ways. Today I am more aware of how synchronicity figures into life and relationships. In addition, I appreciate more fully the challenges of opening oneself to the twists of fate, of exposing oneself to the turning of the wheel of life and of finding meaning in what looks like chance.

My heightened awareness and my thankfulness for the graces that flow from synchronicity have led me to revise this book, to explore further the mysterious power of coincidence in my own life and in those of others. My hope in writing this revised and expanded edition is to share more of what I understand about how all this unfolds and how it blooms.

I am grateful to the staff at Shambhala for believing in this project, and especially to my editor, Eden Steinberg, who attunes so sensitively to my sounds and silences so they can resound more harmoniously.

How sweet the moonlight sleeps upon this bank!
Here will we sit and let the sounds of music
Creep in our ears; soft stillness and the night
Become the touches of sweet harmony.
Sit, Jessica. Look how the floor of heaven
Is thick inlaid with patens of bright gold.
There's not the smallest orb which thou behold'st
But in his motion like an angel sings,
Still quiring to the young-eyed cherubims;
Such harmony is in immortal souls,
But whilst this muddy vesture of decay
Doth grossly close it in, we cannot hear it.
                    —WILLIAM SHAKESPEARE, *The Merchant of Venice*

The Power of Coincidence

Introduction

A series of unusual correspondences or similar happenings may not be mere coincidence but meaningful coincidence. This synchronicity can be just what it takes to spring us into changes and awakenings that we are ready to experience. Synchronous moments bid to us to pay attention to what comes now or next on our journey. From this point of view, awkward jolts can become graceful transitions, and stops can become steps. We grasp that the people, places, and events of our lives are showing us what we need to know or where we are ready to go. Everyone and everything in our story is part of how our life is coming together and there is nothing left to fear. We then stand at attention to our destiny and join it deliberately, rather than resisting, complaining about, or otherwise bemoaning our fate.

If our life unfolded only according to our plans, however sensible or overblown or constricted, we would miss out on many surprises. We might fail to notice how new doors are opening and ushering us into relationships that stretch us and fashion us into works of art. Our life as designed by our cautious mind might not include all the twists and turns that lead to the release of our creative energy or the clash of forces that make us really extraordinary.

Perhaps all is happening in life just as we intend. Then suddenly we meet someone, or find out something, or have an accident, or hit bottom and our world spins in a new direction that ultimately makes all the difference. Those unexpected events beyond our control are the forces of synchronicity that make us who we are—and who we were always meant to be.

Synchronicity is a mind-boggling and sometimes eerie rendezvous between the world and our inner selves. Something happens in the external world and it fits exactly with what we need right now, showing that our human nature and mother nature are two sides of one coin. In nature, each season produces just the conditions that the ecology of the earth requires for its evolutionary growth. Likewise, in our human story, we keep finding just what we require so we can evolve as psychologically healthy and spiritually aware beings. Synchronicity comes to us as an assisting force in this evolution. We are helped in finding ourselves and we help others find themselves. Thus, synchronicity contributes to the joyous fulfillment of our personal destiny in an always luminous world that longs for ever more light.

As synchronicity erases the line between us and nature, it also blurs the line between the timely and the timeless. It underlines moments that reveal eternity to be the ground of our being. When we trust this, we take steps from and on that ground. They are dance steps, not a formal ballet but a mirthful jig, at times indecorous or even irreverent. Actually, everything that happens to us is synchronicity because everything fits perfectly into our step-by-step advance toward a fulfillment of our potential.

Most of us are quite aware of our limited powers and not so aware of our boundless potential. This potential is our true Self, an energy that is unconditionally and universally loving, discerning with the wisdom of the ages, and abundantly rich with healing power. When these sleeping powers are activated, we are acting in accord with the best in us. Our spiritual powers may, however, remain sleeping gi-ants in our psyche and never display themselves in our actions. Then our destiny remains unfulfilled and a sense of something missing may pervade our life. Synchronicity comes along to wake us and fulfill us.

Synchronicity shows us that the world orchestrates some of our life events so they can harmonize with the requirements of our inner journey. This is reflected in the opening quotation by Shakespeare: "Such harmony is in immortal souls." Synchronicities are unusual, unexpected, not constructed or controlled by the human ego. In this sense they are miracles of conjunction between ourselves and the events of the world. We cannot cause these kinds of miracles to occur, but we can greet them and grant them hospitality in the yet-unopened rooms of our souls. Then the power of coincidence is re-spected and it opens us to many marvels. These pages show how that can happen.

The human organism comes equipped with self-healing powers. We have three reliable and highly skilled healers—three graces—within ourselves. The first is an inner physician—the grace of the body—who rushes to the scene of an accident. We cut a finger and he brings platelets to stop the bleeding and white cells to prevent in-fection. We can cooperate in this process by washing and covering the cut—skills we learned from our first aid manual.

We also embody an inner psychologist—the grace of the psy-che—who knows just how to help us with our emotional injuries. When a shocking loss occurs, she brings tears of mourning to the site of the wound. We can join in by actively engaging in griefwork. We can trust our inner psychologist to have a handy program perfectly calibrated for every crisis that may come along. To make that program more effective and expeditious we have to work along with it.

Finally, we are aware of the metaphor of the guardian angel. This is our inner priest, our spiritual guide—the grace of the soul—who knows the full itinerary of our journey through life and can offer the provisions it requires. He brings synchronicity, dreams, intuitions, bursts of imagination, spontaneous creativity, sudden awakenings, and other spiritual gifts. We participate by faithful attention, and then by acting in accord with the callings of our destiny. The skills for this work are presented in this book.

The physical work leads to the joy of health. The psychological work leads to the joy of responsible living and effective relating. The spiritual work leads to the joy of universal love. Our work in all three areas is to synchronize our learned skills with our inborn resources. This is the dance, the harmonized movements of effort and grace that enact the equation of human wholeness. Personal power is an abiding and inviolable trust that the three graces are resident and active in our psyches. It is synchronicity at work—or rather, at play.

My personal purpose in life as a psychotherapist, teacher, and writer is to point to this source in all of us. My books, and most specifically this one, are meant as manuals to assist our inner psychologist and our inner priest in their resplendent work. I am hoping we can build our confidence in the trustworthy light inside us and cultivate the skills to let it come through.

In this book, we learn how to recognize synchronicity in our daily experience, in our imagination, and in our dreams. Such heightened awareness leads to a felt sense about what may be incubating in the hidden depths of our unconscious. We then recognize the crucial significance of timing in all that we do. In these pages I'll draw on the Jungian concept of active imagination, Tibetan Buddhist practices, and other techniques and teachings to help us work with the phenomenon of synchronicity and gain from it. Though I draw strongly on Jungian thought, my intention is not to present Jung's views but to explore what happens when his work is combined with other wisdom traditions including Buddhism, transpersonal psychology, and mystical traditions of spirituality.

Ultimately, this book helps you to learn to "read" synchronicity in your own life so that you can discover:

> How to interpret a series of similar happenings
> How to open yourself to the assisting forces around you
> How to get past the fears that can stop you from being you

How to deal with fate and participate in your own destiny
How to tell the right time from the wrong time
How to use creative imagination in your choices
How to honor and learn from your dreams
How to integrate your psychological and spiritual work
How to live in accord with your deepest needs and wishes

Reading this book will help you to notice the miracles everywhere around and within you. It presents an exciting and yet simple program that gives you a sense of personal efficacy and of spiritual connectedness. Awareness of synchronicity makes you a person of more depth, especially as you see the underlying significance of your story and the world's story as one and the same. This kind of awareness leads to a synchronous, melodic, harmonizing of the music in your soul and the rhythms of the cosmic spheres— which are, of course, one and the same. This is the essence of the speech from *The Merchant of Venice* that appears in the preface of this book, which will be referred to throughout the text. This quotation offers an exquisitely complete and touching articulation of all this book attempts to say.

Synchronicity shows us that more is at work than can be accounted for by chance. Since correlations are happening beyond our control, we trust that something, we know not what, is always at work, we know not how, to make us more than we are now, to make the world more than it is yet.

What a precious and privileged destiny we humans have: to be the escorts of light and love as they enter this world. We are like honor guards in a long procession of forbears and followers, who, like us, are always en route and always already Here.

We spend our lives waiting for the great day, the great battle, or the great deed of power. But that external consummation is not given to many, nor is it necessary. So long as our being is tensed passionately into the spirit in everything, then that spirit will emerge from our own hidden, nameless efforts. . . . Right from the hands that knead the dough to the hands that consecrate it, only one Host is being made.

—PIERRE TEILHARD DE CHARDIN

I

A Moment Becomes Momentum

WHAT IS SYNCHRONICITY?

Synchronicity is a term used by Carl Jung to describe coincidences that are related by meaningfulness rather than by cause and effect. These coincidences are life-affecting and yet beyond our control. Jung saw meaningful coincidence, rather than random chance, as a governing dynamic for all of human experience and history. Thus synchronicity underlies our collective as well as our personal destiny.

We are usually conscious of synchronicity and experience it as mysterious. As we become more attentive to it, we see how our destiny is unfolding and how to take a hand in it. Synchronicity indicates that the timing of events is tied into an unseen pattern of connections. Personally, synchronicity can point us to new challenges or teach us what we need to know. Synchronicity also works in world events to advance human evolution.

Synchronous events include meaningful coincidences, links, correlations, convergences, or correspondences that may guide us, warn us, or confirm us on our path. Synchronicity is also found in a series of similar events or experiences. It can appear as one striking

event that sets off a chain reaction. It is always unexpected and somehow uncanny in its accuracy of connection or revelation. This is what
makes it impossible to dismiss synchronicity as mere coincidence.

In synchronicity, seemingly random events *collaborate* to fashion a
connection that is meaningful to the person it happens to. Jung
wrote of an "acausal connecting principle" in which connections happen by meaning, not by cause-and-effect in the traditional sense.
Quantum physics shows that distantly separated events can indeed be
correlated without there being a direct, physical cause-effect relationship.

How things happen and what will happen form a field of consciousness in which meaningful coincidences occur. What is meaning
and what is a coincidence? Meaningfulness happens when an event or
experience in conscious life puts us in contact with unconscious
forces that lead us to a fulfillment of our destiny. Our destiny is anything that leads to birth, death, finding a life purpose, or awakening
to spiritual consciousness. Coincidence is a bond between two hith-
erto unconnected realities. Synchronicity joins something going on
outside us with something happening inside us. In fact, synchronicity
gives us a clue that there is no real separation between inside and
outside, between internal and external reality. There is continual in-
terplay. In this sense, synchronicity is a spiritual event, one that
shows the unity of human, natural, and divine reality.

Synchronicity is a term based on the Greek words *syn,* meaning "joined with"—that is, connectedness—and *chronos,* meaning
"time." Synchronicity is a bond or connection that happens in a
timely way. A correspondence between two things is suddenly made
clear. The unifying connection was always present but an immediate
and meaningful coincidence makes it visible here and now. Here is an
example: two close childhood friends lose track of one another. As
adults they meet one day by chance and soon thereafter they fall in
love. The meaningful coincidence is in the fact that they were always
meant for each other and met up at just the moment in which they
were ready to know it and act on it.

Coincidence usually refers to something that happens at a specific moment in time. For instance, I arrive at the scene of a crime just in time to intervene and save someone from death. But meaningful links and correspondences can also be ongoing, that is, always present and essential, though often unnoticed. For instance, my minister father is present throughout my childhood as a guide and model, and this leads me to recognize that I too want to pursue a life of service and spirituality. The world of synchronicity thus includes both startling in-the-moment awakenings and quieter, long-term realizations.

An ordinary coincidence may not be synchronicity but simply synchronization, that is, simultaneity. Here is a simple example of the difference between synchronicity and synchronization: I am afraid to dive and while at the pool, I see a father teaching his son to dive. I am touched by the tenderness I see in the dad and the gracefulness in his way of diving. I watch and learn and somehow let go of my fear. This was a simple coincidence, synchronization of need and resource. Later, because of my learning to dive, my confidence builds and I eventually become a diving teacher, start a diving school, and even help an Olympic hopeful. I can trace this fulfilling work back to my first eavesdropping and experimenting at the pool. This makes that original event synchronicity. I always had it in me to dive; I learned to do it at a specific moment. This is how the essential ongoing fact became an existential, here and now, reality. Adding to the meaning, I find that in ancient times, diving from a high cliff was an initiatory sacrament, representing a plunge into the unknown waters of rebirth, a primitive form of baptism. This enriches my sense of my spiritual work. Now the synchronicity has reached me more deeply and the grace of it has appeared more clearly. I have entered the realm of the miraculous.

Indeed, synchronicity cannot happen by any conscious intervention of ego since it is a phenomenon of grace, an arrival of the transpersonal world onto our home turf. It is a moment that manifests the unity that always and already existed between psychological and spiritual, mind and universe, you and me, we and everything. It occurs when something unconscious is ready for a step up into consciousness.

Carl Jung described synchronicity as "a noncausal but meaningful relationship between physical and psychic events. . . . A special instance of acausal orderedness. . . . Conscious succession becomes simultaneity. . . . Synchronicity takes the events in space and time as meaning more than mere chance." Synchronicity is thus the opposite of cause/effect connections. In synchronicity, the link is forged by meaningfulness, not by linear reaction of cause to effect. Since the Self—the larger life in us and in the universe that transcends ego and separateness—is not bound by linear time, it can use another model for succession. Instead of an effect following a cause, there can also be instances in which things happen together. Simultaneity takes the place of linear progression in the timeless world of the psyche. Synchronicity is the word for this alternative. To say that something transcends cause/effect means it is beyond ego control, another clue to the Self at work.

THE MANY WAYS IT CAN HAPPEN

Synchronicities cluster around significant events, both personal and historical. They can be felt by us as positive or negative in their impact. Many meaningful coincidences occurred, for instance, when the Titanic sank and when presidents Lincoln and Kennedy were assassinated. Some passengers signed on to the Titanic voyage against their better judgment; some failed to appear for the voyage; some took someone else's place; some cancelled their reservations because of premonitions of danger. The assassinations of Presidents Lincoln and Kennedy include a number of coincidences. In both instances their wives were present; both their successors were named Johnson and were Southern senators; both assassins were themselves killed before a trial could occur; Booth shot Lincoln in a theater and escaped to a warehouse, while Oswald fired at Kennedy from a warehouse and ran into a theater.

On a personal level, Norma orders a red dress for a party but a black dress is delivered to her. As she is about to phone the store to report the error, her sister calls: "Mother has died. Come for the funeral." Norma thought she was in control of her life; she thought she knew what would happen next and what she would need. The synchronous event told her otherwise and outfitted her for what was actually coming next; something much more momentous was about to occur. Synchronicity is the surprise that something unplanned or unwanted suddenly fits.

Synchronicity also works directly or symbolically in a dream, intuition, or premonition. They may speak to an existing life situation and present a useful meaning to it. Synchronicity occurs in a dream that reveals what is already true or about to become true. Lincoln dreamed he would be assassinated one week before the tragedy. As we shall see, dreams and astrology manifest many synchronous correspondences.

Consecutive events in life constitute the exterior order of our existence. An interior order manifests in dreams and synchronicity, which show us the hidden acausal order of things. Sudden intuitions or moments of truth are synchronous because they represent explicating moments in which a deeper meaning of our life becomes visible. The function of intuition is to reveal the vast field of possibility in this one moment of insight. Intuition is thus a springboard to the release of our inner immense potential.

We may see synchronicity also in the fact that within our human collective is a tendency to make similar discoveries around the same historical time. We recall the theory of "morphic resonance" as proposed by biologist Rupert Sheldrake. Monkeys on different islands begin a new practice: washing yams before eating them. This occurs almost simultaneously when there is no way for the diverse groups of monkeys to share information. The world of nature has connections that transcend time and place, and this is precisely where synchronicity resides.

Synchronicity can take the form of the coincidence of a psychic perception and a simultaneously occurring event, as happens in ESP.

Premonitions are in this category. An example of synchronous premonition is given by Jung about a patient of his with many phobias. All were cleared in therapy except for one, his fear of walking on outdoor stairs. The patient was later killed by a stray bullet from a street fight on just such stairs. This was synchronicity, a premonition of a significant truth—not a phobia after all. (Or perhaps the phobia was a long-standing self-protective device!)

Déjà vu is the illusory belief that something happening in the present was already experienced in the past. (If it indeed happened, it is a memory, not déjà vu.) It is synchronicity when it represents a meaningful connection to a past moment that is still unfinished in our psyches and now suddenly makes a haunting plea for our attention.

Synchronicity sometimes pieces itself together over days or months or even years: I was climbing in the mountains of Crete a few years ago noticing echoes and the eerie reverberations of the winds, when I suddenly realized that they had a *voice*. A month later, I was climbing to the top of Mount Sinai and I remembered that Moses heard a voice that drew him up this mountain. "That was the voice I must have felt in the mountains of Crete," I thought. That evening, I was sitting with Father Paul, one of the monks of Saint Catherine's monastery at the foot of Mount Sinai. He said, "The mountains pray." I felt that the voice was now speaking to me, asking me to hear it or even to find my voice in its own.

Our answered prayers are another manifestation of synchronicity since prayers that are fulfilled are the ones that are consistent with our destiny. Some miraculous events described in religious traditions may be synchronicities. For example, in the story of the exodus, the Israelites arrived at the Red Sea just as the winds were blowing open a path through it. The Egyptians found the waters rising again to their dismay. This is synchronicity for the Jews and asynchrony—"the time is out of joint"—for the Egyptians.

Synchronicity represents a perfect paradox. A paradox is an apparent contradiction that is nonetheless true. There is an apparent contradiction between multiplicity and unity. Yet, in synchronicity, two events become one in significance. The existential display of two circumstances, one of which may be external and one internal, are essentially one in meaningful design. An analogy might be found in medieval herbalism. The "law of signatures" referred to the similarity between certain plants and parts of the human body. It was believed that this resemblance meant that the herb had healing qualities for that organ. In homeopathy, "the law of similars" is also an example: one is healed by what ails one. In both instances, similitude and symmetry are vehicles to wholeness.

Synchronicity is always striking and sometimes eerie. Our "other worldly" sense when it happens to us may be an indicator that an archetypal meaning is arising into consciousness from the depths of our psyche. This can also be a religious experience since our ordinary consciousness is being touched and moved by transcendence. Jung comments in *Memories, Dreams, Reflections:* "In the end, the only events in life worth telling are those in which the imperishable world erupted into this transitory world."

The archetypal, collective Self of humanity is a field of perpetual possibility in time and of infinite possibility in space. Its potential is in the vast extent of its love, wisdom, and healing power, in individual people and in all of nature. For these potentials to be actualized in us, three creative commitments are required from our ego. We can learn to love generously. We can access intuitive wisdom by transcending logical categories. We can bring balance and reconciliation to the world and to human relationships by letting go of retaliation. Synchronicity is a message from the higher Self to the ego about how to effect this and grants opportunities to practice it.

Synchronicity thus reveals a deep underlay of purpose and meaning in the universe and shows how that purpose is working itself out in and through our lives. Thus the realization of human wholeness has a foundation and support in the larger order of things. Objective events have a corresponding subjective resonance in our psyche. Synchronicity is an instant instance of this correspondence. The tale of the meaningful bond between the subjective and objective world is told by synchronicity. Its spontaneous timely events are articulations of the irrefragable unity guessed at in poetry, Buddhism, and universal religious mysticism.

STORIES THAT REVEAL SYNCHRONICITY

Here are some examples of synchronicity on historic and personal levels.

Synchronicity characterizes the journey toward enlightenment.

Prince Gautama was born into just the family that would shield him from the real world so that his curiosity would later lead him to explore it. In one visit beyond the palace walls, he discovered the realities of human suffering: sickness, old age, and death. The prince then turned to asceticism as his spiritual path. This became so extreme that he endangered his health. One day he was given a bowl of rice milk by a young girl and he realized the wisdom of moderation, the middle path. He sat under a fig tree in perfect meditation, open to enlightenment, and it finally happened.

Dogen Zenji reports his enlightenment experience as synchronicity: "When the morning star appeared, I and the great earth with all its beings simultaneously became Buddhas." Each event of Gautama's life pieced together a path to awakening. Each event of our life is synchronicity as it lines up to make enlightenment possible in any and every moment.

Synchronicity appears in a single, sometimes painful, occurrence that sets off a chain of events that work out for the best:

Joseph in the Old Testament was sold into slavery to the Egyptians by his brothers. He rose in power in Egypt because of his skill in dream interpretation and because of his personal integrity. In accord with his interpretation of the Pharaoh's dream, he prepared for and headed off a disaster from a future famine. When his brothers, many years later, felt the effects of this same famine, they came to Joseph and he was able to feed them and be reconciled with his family.

Synchronicity is found in an event that seems meaningless when it happens but later shows itself to be of utmost significance:

Abraham Lincoln, out of compassion for a man who was forced to sell all he had, bought a barrel from him for his asking price of one dollar. Lincoln never asked what it contained. He stored it at home and forgot about it. Later on, Lincoln went through a long period of confusion and indecision about whether to enter the legal profession or that of journalism. In the midst of this quandary, he happened to notice the barrel and lackadaisically opened it. It contained a set of law books. He took this as a sign and entered the profession that led to politics and the presidency. The many synchronicities in Lincoln's life—and in the lives of most great people—show so emphatically how synchronicity points to destiny.

Synchronicity can arise in the form of a dream that answers a waking-world question or in a dream that foretells the future:

Elias Howe, in the nineteenth century, invented the sewing machine. However, he could not figure out how to shape the needle to let the thread run through it and simultaneously through the material being sewed. He pondered long and hard with no results. Without such a needle, the invention was useless. One night, Elias, who lived in Massachusetts, dreamed he was in Africa observing natives with strange spears. He was drawn to the unusual shape of the blades with an oblong hole in the center. When Howe awoke, he realized he had found the solution to his problem.

Synchronicity shows itself in sudden or spontaneous decisions that we make, not knowing why, that later prove significant:

Fritz Perls, the founder of Gestalt therapy, taught in a university in Germany in the thirties. He and two of his colleagues were asked one day by their department chair if any one of them would like a transfer to teach at the German university in South Africa. The two colleagues began asking questions about the practical aspects of the move but Perls immediately said "Yes." All three of them were Jewish and within a few short years, the two colleagues were in concentration camps while Perls remained safe in Africa. Later, he came to America and made important contributions to the field of psychotherapy.

Synchronicity occurs in an unusual coincidence that later proves to be necessary or helpful:

In Nebraska, several years ago, every member of a church choir failed to show up for choir practice on the very night the furnace blew up. Their lives were saved by this unusual coincidence. Prior to that night, each member had appeared faithfully and punctually every week without exception.

Synchronicity can appear as a response to a question about the future or about the reality of a spiritual world:

One evening, my friend's cousin, Concetta, a middle-aged woman, whose mother had died recently, was sitting with her father in the house where she had grown up. Her husband would be coming later to pick her up to return to their home. As her father dozed off, Concetta was reminiscing about her mother and was wondering if there were a heaven or any afterlife. Suddenly, she found herself saying, "Ma, if there is another world, send me a slice of pizza." Shortly thereafter, Concetta's husband called from a pizzeria to tell her he would not be able to pick her up but that her brother would come instead. She said, "That's fine" and was about to hang up when Tony added, "And, by the way, he's bringing you a slice of pizza."

There is synchronicity in the way we find our destiny in life through people and events:

Mother Teresa was born in Albania. At age fifteen, she heard of women who worked among the poor as missionaries. She was filled with an ardent desire to do that work. At eighteen, never having seen a nun, she left home for Ireland and joined the Sisters of Loreto, missionaries to India. Soon Mother Teresa indeed found herself teaching in Calcutta, but the convent and school were behind a wall and served rich girls, and she was not allowed to work in the slums where she felt called to be. At age thirty-eight, she was released by special permission of the Pope to fulfill her dream. She felt a deep loneliness as she worked all by herself as a teacher of the poor with no money, supplies, or sisterly support. One day, Mother Teresa saw a dying woman and stayed by her on the street. This expanded her sense of her mission and she began nursing the sick and dying. One nun joined her. Now there are thousands of nuns and lay people continuing her work. Her destiny in the world began as a wish and ended in a work that helped those with needs and mobilized those with resources. Just the meetings and events occurred to make it all happen as she, and the world, needed it to happen.

There is synchronicity in the way a physical disability and/or an emotional wound becomes the threshold to our mission in life or to the unfolding of our talents. The wounded healer archetype thrives on this synchronicity:

Helen Keller's own hardships became precisely what it took for her to find her destiny of service to others. And in the film, *My Left Foot,* we saw another example: Christy Brown was afflicted with cerebral palsy and unable to use his hands. He successfully used his left foot to express his talent in painting and writing.

In our own lives we may have been abused in childhood and now could ask ourselves how this has helped us become bolder within ourselves and more compassionate toward others. "Because I was neglected, I learned to be self-sufficient. Because I was left out, I am more conscious of including others now." Our wounds are often the openings into the best and most beautiful part of us. We all recall the cruel stepmother in fairy tales. That archetype is often a necessary element in a fairy tale so that the heroine/hero can become a person of character and power. Stories of heroes and heroines often begin with a wound or loss or injustice and end with heroic acts of restoration and gift-bestowing love: "It takes just such evil and painful things for the great emancipation to occur," Nietzsche says.

Synchronicity can open us to our psychological work or to our sense of a world beyond rational scientific thought:

One of Carl Jung's patients was a young woman who was resistant to his form of transpersonal, archetypal treatment because she was so much "in her head." One day she shared a dream in which she was handed a golden scarab. As Jung listened to her, he was distracted by the tapping of a beetle at his window. He opened the window and it flew into the room. It was a *Scarabaeidae* beetle, a close equivalent of the scarab in his patient's dream. Both Jung and the young woman could see the synchronicity in that event and she became more open to the spiritual dimension of life.

Synchronicity is at work when something occurs that substantiates a belief or philosophy of life.

There is a touching story told by Jung in *The Archetypes and the Collective Unconscious* of an event that fit and confirmed his belief that humans always hoped in an afterlife. Another point in this story is its affirmation of the power of love:

> In Upper Egypt, near Aswan, I once looked into an ancient Egyptian tomb that had just been opened. Just behind the entrance door was a little basket made of reeds, containing the withered body of a newborn infant, wrapped in rags. Evidently the wife of one of the workmen had hastily laid the body of her dead child in the nobleman's tomb at the last moment. She must have hoped that, when the great man entered the sun barge in order to rise anew, the little stowaway might share in his salvation, because it was in the holy precinct within reach of divine grace.

Learning to Practice Openness to Synchronicity

Synchronicity invites or challenges us to become more capable of loving, of accessing wisdom, of becoming a source of healing and peace. The actualization of these potentials *is* our spiritual destiny. We do not create our destiny; we participate in its unfolding. Synchronicity works as a catalyst toward the working out of that destiny. It can help us in this way because it is a numinous visit of the transcendent/transpersonal into our transitory/personal world. These are worlds that love to embrace. Synchronicity is thus a major tool of soul-making, divulging immortal meanings through personal events so that we can find our way toward integration. We can find this way through practices.

The suggestions that follow, like all those in this book, are meant to help you work *with* synchronicity in two ways: You learn to recognize synchronicities and follow them up with practices that take their cues, always uniquely designed by your higher Self to move you toward your destiny of wholeness. Consider each of these elements of synchronicity and ask which ones are afoot right now in your life. Make a conscious choice to become aware of these as they happen in the near future.

> Coincidence, correspondence, connection, resemblance, links between past events or meetings and later developments
>
> Triggers to a series of events or turning points
>
> The unexpected, unusual, uncanny, improbable
>
> What happens on the spur of the moment and just in time
>
> What is meaningful, revelatory, and has become conscious to us
>
> What happens beyond our control or contrary to our wishes
>
> The fluke or choice or happenstance that uncovers a whole new possibility in our psyche or a path to our true bliss or calling
>
> Serendipity, finding good fortune by accident, a way of referring to the playful dimension of synchronicity

In what follows, and in all the practices recommended in this book, use art, sculpture, music-composing, poetry, dance, or any art form that is appealing to you.

1. Keep track in your journal of any coincidences that happen as you read this book. Notice which of them become meaningful, that is, bring out the best in you; change your perspective in such a way that new things can happen to you; or

make you more loving, or wiser, or more able to help or heal yourself or others. Find a personal message from these experiences, one that moves you along on your journey. This happens when you challenge yourself to act in new ways, to go out of character, to be more authentic about your deepest needs and wishes, and to have a sense of personal mission.

If you do not have a spiritual teacher or mentor, share your experiences with the friend who seems most spiritually conscious and listen to his/her feedback. Take the feedback as an extension of the synchronicity that touched off this process of finding your own mission. What purpose of the universe wants to work itself out in you? How has it already begun? How have you participated in it or sabotaged it?

2. Look at the significant events in your life, listing them by decade, and explore the synchronicities that may have happened around them. What message was trying to come through? Look at events that seemed negative at first and then turned into something good. What synchronicities clustered around those events? Now look at your present life. If synchronicity happens around an event that seems negative to you now, there may be something positive in the works. Find something good in what seems so bad and look for ways to expand on it.

3. Pay attention to the surprises that happen to you. What do they call you to uncover? Are you setting up your life so that there will be no surprises? Is everything too orderly? What do you lose that way? Is fear behind your not being surprised very much these days?

4. What are some correspondences, similarities, or serendipities that have happened this month? How do they warn, guide, or confirm you? What may be afoot in your life? What new freedom in you may be endeavoring to be born by lightening you of what you have been carrying for so long? Perhaps there are obligations that you want to be done with. Or

perhaps there are things you may be loath to lose, but the time has come to let them go.

5. What are the images—or one image—that come up over and over for you? How do they point to something you are ready to go for or to let go of? Is there a need or want in you that is not being fulfilled? Does not the synchronicity of an image continually fascinating you call you to follow it through? Look at your dream images too. What do the images and synchronicities say to you about your present predicament?

6. Every coincidence offers a grace. Notice how, in the stories above, an increase of consciousness led to an increase in love, wisdom, and/or healing. Look at your own experiences of synchronicity to find the very same possibility.

7. The next time you experience déjà vu, ask what is unfinished that is asking for closure, or what loss you are regretting, or what era of life you might like to return to in order to begin again at that point. How does any of this elicit grief or its milder friend, nostalgia?

8. Has there been a series of similar events—or dreams—in the past month or two? What is the common theme? What force beyond yourself is trying to reach you through this orchestration of your life? What challenge does this theme present to you? What is exciting about it? What scares you? Write out the answers to these questions and notice which feelings arise in you. How do these feelings help or hinder you in responding to the theme?

9. Most people have some powers of premonition or ESP. When have they displayed themselves in the course of your life? For most people, they arise more emphatically when something is brewing within. Do you notice yourself becoming more sensitive when major changes or transitions are afoot? The more attention you pay to the powers—no matter how minor—the more they will increase. Inner power is a guest that loves to visit a welcoming host.

INTERPRETING SYNCHRONICITIES

A series of:	*May mean that it is time to:*
Losses	Let go
Opportunities	Take hold
Informative facts being revealed	Take heed or break through denial
Failures to locate information	You do not need to know yet or at all
False accusations	Let go of the need to impress
Many things going wrong	Step back
Physical breakdowns	Pay attention to your stresses
Transitions that happen with ease	You are on track
Embarrassments	Deflate ego
The same old problems	This is where your work is
Betrayals	Relocate your trust
Memories	Let yourself grieve
Opportunities to be generous	Let go of attachment and clinging

A disclaimer is appropriate here: a series of losses may also call for *effort* instead of letting go. In fact, every entry above may be reversed. A synchronicity may feel like something that is "meant to be" when it is really "meant to beware!" There is no reliable chart or pilot when it comes to navigating the seas of change and synchronicity. It is our call. Therefore, a danger in considering synchronicity is to project a meaning where there is none in order to fulfill our own ego need to feel special. We might also see coincidences in a paranoid way, imagining others are either plotting against us or venerating us. It is wise to share our interpretations of synchronicities with those we trust to get objective feedback or to confirm our groundedness.

Using the list above, carefully examine your life in the past six months and write down events, choices, and activities that fit for each of the above entries. Notice where the preponderance of your responses fall. What is happening in your life now? Are you visiting one side exclusively? How can you balance yourself so that you visit both sides? Are you holding on when it is time to let go? Are you hanging in when it is time to get out? Have you noticed that sometimes the metaphor of a door closing and a window opening has come true for you?

In the introduction, we met the three graces within us: physician, psychologist, and priest or guide. Consider therapy with a spiritually conscious therapist as part of the work that synchronicity points to. Therapists assist the client's inner psychologist and inner guide in their luminous work. They help build confidence in the trustworthy light within a person and foster the skills to let it come through. As a client you have something working for you that is as wise as Freud or Jung. Therapists can invite that interior resource out and then facilitate your follow-up skills. When a therapist sits with a client, the therapist is not alone in a berth with a hapless stowaway. She is on the upper deck, the realm of the higher Self, with an unrecognized master navigator (inner psychologist and guide) in an untrained sailor afraid of the voyage ahead but wanting to make it happen. With all of these forces working together, we voyagers build confidence and learn the ropes of life. Then the rigging can be nimbly handled and the rich port reached.

Every synchronicity in my life is just such a bridge.

2

How Synchronicity Touches Us and Our Relationships

There are many events in the womb of time which will be delivered.
—WILLIAM SHAKESPEARE, *Othello*

Synchronicity is the strikingly meaningful coincidence of two events or of a series of events. The case can be made for synchronicity only if meaningfulness is present. That is always the ultimate criterion of synchronicity, and it happens only when we notice it. Noticing meanings in ourselves and in our relationships is the beginning of working on ourselves because we become conscious rather than unmindful.

Synchronicity may appear in a specific symptom we now face, in a depression we find ourselves caught in, in a quandary that obsesses us. We may find in any of these painful experiences a new potential for self-healing or a new direction on our life path. There is a healing predisposition in the psyche to produce just the spurs we need and just in time. The object relations expert Margaret Mahler wrote, "There is in us an innate given, a thrust toward individuation." A symptom arises from that thrust and healing means finding a path to individuation because of it. *Individuation* is the term Jung used to describe the lifelong process by which we become who we really are: our inner wholeness becomes visible; our potentials are realized; ego and Self form an axis. The result is psychologically effective and spiritually enlightened living.

Synchronicity certainly appears in our work on ourselves by the very fact that our knowledge of our real issues comes simultaneously with relationships that expose them. We are usually oblivious or in denial for a long time before we finally recognize and acknowledge the truth of who we are. When we do, we find strength to look more deeply into ourselves and find courage to face our demons and our angels too. Synchronicity appears in the fact that we often only let ourselves know something about ourselves or others when we can deal with what we know.

Our inner healers—the physician, psychologist, and priestly guide whom we met in the introduction—work synchronously in providing resources tailored to our needs. We join in synchronously when we use the skills that correlate to our innate healing inclinations and make it one cooperative rendezvous of grace and effort. We match our daily skills to the healing course of action always and already in progress in the self-restorative psyche.

How we meet future partners is usually synchronicity at work in our lives. Two people both love whale-watching and join an expedition from their local pier on the same Sunday afternoon. That is a coincidence. Unknown to each other, they strike up a conversation while they are both leaning over the side of the boat to observe the whales cavorting in the waves. Based on their common interest, they plan a date and soon fall in love. After a courtship, they are married. The boat trip is synchronicity as is the leaning together side by side to see the whales since these events started a lifetime together. Their mutual love of whale-watching prepared them to find their life's fulfillment in relationship. A chance meeting was not chance but grace. An unusual interest was a path to happiness.

We might also say that every experience of falling in love or of entering an intimate relationship is an example of synchronicity since we inevitably meet just the people who teach us what we need to learn about life, love, and ourselves. We meet the people on whom we can transfer the needs and expectations related to our childhood. We bond with the person who will show us what we have not worked through from our past and who will help us complete our unfinished emotional business, if we are willing to do the work it takes for that to happen.

In fact, synchronicity often happens because of a link between a new contact with someone and what follows later that turns out to be important to us. We may meet just the person who shows us our hidden potential for art, for a profession, or for a skill. Someone uncovers an orientation in us in the area of sex or a hobby or even a spiritual practice. Someone shows us what is really going on politically and we join or find a cause to believe in. Over and over in life we are meeting exactly the people who help us wake up to what is dormant in ourselves. It can happen on a blind date, in a chance meeting, at a lecture we are dragged to, at a mistaken address, and in the "chemistry" between ourselves and someone else from which a romance or marriage may result.

Synchronicity sometimes reveals a truth about our relationship in words that prove to be true in a larger sense than ever we intended: "Little did I know then!" We may state something humorously or figuratively and if we think about it more carefully, we realize it has precisely that meaning literally. For instance, you ask me how my stormy relationship is going and I say, "Things are sort of patched up." Later, I find myself returning to that phrase and realize that it describes the exact nature of my relationship. Things are never resolved or changed, only patched up. I have opened myself to my own truth by a Freudian slip of synchronicity.

The thrust toward wholeness/individuation makes us apt to place ourselves in relationships that help us complete the unfinished business of childhood. Past events and childhood relationships register in our psyches with the laconic vocabulary of ants: "done or undone?" Undone in the human context refers to issues that are still unaddressed, unprocessed, or unresolved. We locate in our present life relationships just the people who resemble past significant figures and they play their parts as we work out our archaic dramas. This happens in unconscious projection or transference, both forms of synchronicity since they perfectly match a new person we meet with our readiness to finish our own old business. Transference assigns parental meanings onto an adult partner. Projection makes us see in others what is disavowed in ourselves, both positively in our untapped potential and negatively in our hidden unacceptable traits and wishes. The overarching yearning for wholeness in our psyches is the genesis of transference and projection. They are useful when we make them conscious and work at what they point us to.

Indeed, everyone and every event in life's drama is part of the metaphor of our journey. The issue from an old relationship may not be "How bad he was" but "How much I needed to learn!" Most of us keep meeting partners who show us exactly where our work is. Our wounds are openings into our missing life. Often, the only way a lost piece of ourselves or of our history comes back to us is through another person. The unknown is scary, *so just the right people and events come along that help us go there.* This is synchronicity. The only mistake we make is hanging on to some people too long or too briefly. We take them as literally themselves instead of as themselves *and* metaphorical forces come to boost or chide.

"We meet those to whom we belong in the world of the Self," says Marie-Louise Von Franz. There is synchronicity in how we unerringly find exactly the people who show us to ourselves. Events occur that provide the same service. A spiritually conscious response might be: "If *this* is happening to me, it can be one of the ingredients of my destiny. The only thing that can get in the way is my own ego, not the events that occur or the people who bring them. The force of grace brought me here." Virgil wrote about a sad event: "Someday it will help to remember even this."

THE EXPERIENCES AND EVENTS THAT BROUGHT US HERE

In addition to our meeting remarkable persons, we also meet up with exactly the experiences that open or awaken us. It can happen through a book that is life-changing, a blunder that hurls an unexpected advantage toward us, a loss that makes room for new possibilities, an opportunity that was meant for someone else and came our way, a plan that failed and became a boon unhoped for, an accident that disabled us, a disaster that devastated us, a windfall that gratified us, a rejection by one person followed by an unexpected appreciation by another, something crossing our path that disturbs or profits us, everything falling into place, or the luck of the draw. Fortunately for us, any person, place, or thing is a possible point of departure for new vistas and more light to see them by. The Big Bang as a point of departure for the world means that our whole existence began with synchronicity.

There is synchronicity in the events of the day that create a strong reaction in us. They are metaphors for deeper unacknowledged feelings and unfinished emotional business that may be calling for attention. For example, being overly upset about being delayed behind a school bus may be a metaphor for something holding up the traffic on our life journey. We are living behind an obstacle over which we have no control. Then we see the choice to become more of a controller or more of a listener. This is openness, a readiness to learn.

When we are ready to learn, a teacher appears. This is synchronicity and can occur with the living or the dead. Occasionally, a person who died long ago or recently comes to our mind over and over in the course of a week or more. It could be that the meaning of that person in our life is coming home to us in a compelling way. Perhaps we learned something from that person and need to remember it now. This may be another form of synchronicity. The face of the teacher appears when the time has come to be instructed or to gain a deeper insight into who we are. This might even be the time to ask that person to be our guide if that fits our worldview.

Those who guide and teach are also touched by synchronicity. Therapists may notice that clients seem to appear presenting just the issues that they themselves most need to work on. Teachers are asked just the questions they may need to ask themselves. Writers may be writing about just what they most need to focus on in their own lives.

Synchronicity activates and enlivens us when there is a significant coincidence between what happens to us and our internal readiness for a change or a transition. As I am in a letting go phase, losses happen. In my challenge phase, opportunities and oppositions happen. To integrate is to go with what wants to happen, not stopping the momentum of that which I cannot change but riding it, jumping on the train just as it comes through the station. Trust is always an invaluable companion on the synchronous track. Our work is then to capitalize on conscious choice moments that match inner unconscious momentum.

Some events are meaningful coincidences in that they touch off a chain reaction, for example, a painful loss leads eventually to a surprisingly positive outcome. We may not know how what is happening right now really fits into our future. "We do not know whether the things afflicting us are the secret beginning of our happiness or not," wrote Jorge Borges. We can only trust that in addition to all that we see, there is some other vision that will appear and make all this appear as just right for our growth. A spiritual practice of trust and openness is necessary if synchronicity is to be appreciated.

There is a special synchronicity in suddenly saying Yes to an offer or experience that would ordinarily be out of character for us to assent to. We break through an inhibition or a fear and suddenly we find ourselves in a new unexplored world that challenges and stretches us. And lo, this new realm accurately reflects our deepest needs and wishes. A whole new chapter opens in our lives because of a chance change. The *yes* to something that anytime before would have received a *no* was synchronicity within us taking us beyond our limits. Whoever made the original invitation was an assisting force, a grace in person.

Grace is the higher power than ego at work in synchronicity. This power seems to have heart, that is, to want what is best for our growth. This follows from the fact that synchronous events usually present just the challenges that make for our personal progress and for that of our planet. Since so many significant events of our lives happen in unplanned, synchronous ways, we can trust the universe to be in on our journey to venture beyond the limitations of our controlling ego. The eternal present makes an appearance in the momentary present. This is why it seems fitting to say that synchronicity guides us into spirituality.

Synchronicity is found also in the coincidence of an image we have held onto with fascination over the years and some piece of our work on ourselves for which it is a metaphor. Anything that has gripped and enriched us has a larger meaning than we may guess. If all my life I have been in awe of the shapes and subtleties of seashells, there is probably a lesson or an assistance (physical, psychological, or spiritual) that will come to me precisely at the time I need it from the presence or image of shells. Dostoevsky says, "It must have lain hidden in my soul, though I knew nothing of it, and it rose suddenly to my memory when it was needed." Images held onto with fascination are thereby assisting forces. Blisses are too! "When you follow your bliss," Joseph Campbell says, "doors open where there were no doors before!" That is synchronicity. And, when bliss meets talent, behold the synchronicity of finding a vocation.

The quotation from Dostoevsky can also refer to how we may not notice that an activity, learning, or project we have been engaged in will come in handy later in an unexpected way. Synchronicity is at work when our actions turn out to be preparations we have unwittingly made to handle a future need. For instance, we keep reading a poster in the restroom at work about how to perform the Heimlich maneuver and then, at a family dinner, we use it to save our aunt from choking. We join a *sangha* or faith group and engage in spiritual practices and soon thereafter we face a crisis and all of that shores us up well. We volunteer at a hospice and, when our spouse dies suddenly, its services are there for us.

In synchronicity a coincidence makes a meaningful connection between our vocation and our destiny. Our destiny is to evolve, to be fulfilled, to become self-realized, and to share our unique gifts. Some of our gifts are talents, skills, and aptitudes, psychological and physical. Our spiritual gifts are showing love unconditionally, seeing and acting wisely, and bringing healing to ourselves and our world. To have gifts means they are given. Thus we are receiving the help of assisting forces, graces that our ego's power cannot construct on its own. Synchronicity is one of those forces of grace. It is the spur of the moment in that it spurs us on and it happens just in time for us to learn or make a move or grow in some new way. Synchronicity is also *just* in time in the sense that it is part of the justice of the evolutionary universe in bringing us exactly the pieces we need to fashion—or be fashioned by—our destiny.

Synchronicity can also be recognized as we look back upon our life and notice how it all prepared us or instructed us for the fullest fruition of our potential. A hidden feeling or truth waited to be awakened by just the right person or circumstance, sometimes painfully. "My wounds are making me a wounded healer. My Jewish background has led me to take action against genocides everywhere on the globe. My neglectful father helped me practice for the independent life I live now. My destiny had to have just such a beginning." James Hillman writes, "This way of seeing removes the burden from the early years as having been a mistake and yourself a victim of handicaps and cruelties; instead it is the acorn in the mirror."

A DARK SIDE

There is negative synchronicity in world events that bring destruction because of a dangerous or tragic coincidence in time, place, or decision. For example, the iceberg that destroyed the Titanic began to form fifteen thousand years ago. In 1909, while the ship was being constructed, it broke off from Greenland and began to move toward the North Atlantic. Unusually, it traveled as far south as the latitude of New York City. In April 1912 it crossed paths with the Titanic, resulting in the deaths of fifteen hundred passengers. The captain had decided to speed up the voyage. If the ship had kept to its original schedule, it would not have collided with the iceberg that was steadily moving toward no particular destination.

Two terrifying negative synchronicities have appeared in our contemporary world. We see country after country engaging in wars and terrorism and proud of having nuclear weaponry. Secondly, we see a rise in fundamentalism and religious fanaticism all over the world. Both these threats to planetary stability seem unstoppable by the forces that speak up against them. The prophetic voices are heard but not believed, and they remain marginal in any case. At the same time, there is certainly a rise in spiritual consciousness among people everywhere. Part of this is owing to the negative synchronicity of China's attack on Tibet triggering exile for so many monks and teachers. This led to the positive synchronicity of Buddhism coming to the West in a stronger way than ever before. All these events are happening at the same time. Negative and positive synchronicity seem to be meeting, but we do not yet see a convergence in favor of sanity and the arts of peace and cooperation.

Consider an example that is more personal: You meet someone who captivates you. By synchronicity you meet up with him again and again. You are excited and you presume this is the force of destiny. You believe he is your soul mate but in reality he is the trickster who takes all you have and leaves you flat. There was indeed a connection between you but it was not destiny. It was karma. You met him so you could learn something, not so that you could live happily ever after in his embrace. This appears to be negative synchronicity but becomes positive when you gain knowledge of yourself from your experience, learn not seek to revenge but let go, and of course, become more careful the next time.

PRACTICING BEGINNER'S MIND

1. List the things you are finding out about yourself from this book and from the synchronicities of your recent life. For instance, if a series of losses have occurred, has it been difficult or easy to grieve and let go? Usually, when we are ready to know where our work is, we are ready to begin doing it. The work consists of addressing, processing, and hopefully, thereby resolving what has come up. As you move through this book, you will be gathering skills that will help you in that enterprise. Begin today by reading your list aloud and saying, "Yes, this did happen. Yes, I have something to learn from it. Yes, I am willing to stay focused on this and to feel the feelings that come up around it." Even if you are not ready to do all this today, you are beginning the process, and having that beginner's mind alone is success. Form an image of your inner psychologist and your inner guide and ask their assistance in the ongoing project of living a more and more conscious and self-expanding life.

2. Consider the problem or symptom that nags at you physically or emotionally. It may be a synchronous repetition that symbolizes a deep cry or longing that you have failed to acknowledge. Give it a hearing and follow what it says. Do this by dialoguing with the symptom or problem in written form. Look particularly for the gift dimension of the symptom that plagues you. Since we contain all apparent opposites, there is a valuable kernel in even the most hard-shell suffering. It might be in a lesson that you learn. It might be in the opening of a new room in your psyche, a new space for a deeper look at yourself. It might be in the engendering of compassion for others who suffer as you do.

3. Notice the circular self-negating phrases from your parents that you keep hearing in your head. Notice those you say most often to your children or partner. How are these true in a larger sense than is found in the literal meaning? How do

these verdicts dictate your life choices, your manner with others, and your self-image? How can they be redesigned so that they are healing? What are the positive hurrahs you heard in childhood and the ones you say to others now? Which of my choices this week are based on obligation or fear and which flow from bliss?

4. What you have wanted to be all your life may be synchronous with what the universe needs from you to fulfill your destiny of happiness and the capacity to give to others what only you can give. What has held you back from going for it? What has propelled you toward it? Thank the people who encouraged your self-emergence. Let yourself feel anger, but not blame, toward those who interfered with your achievement of your life goals. What will it take for you to let go of blame and shame and to move on under your own steam? Are you saying to yourself that it is too late? If you are, picture Grandma Moses now and tell her that in your mind. She began painting in her seventies and died at one hundred and one!

As I settle into the reality of who I am, with pride in my gifts and unabashed awareness of my limits, I notice that I feel lighter and happier.

SYNCHRONICITY AND MIRRORING LOVE

Only in the arms of someone can the first "I am" be pronounced, or rather, risked.

—D. W. WINNICOTT

A profoundly personal form of synchronicity is in mirroring in early life. Mirroring is a pleased and gracious acceptance of an infant by a mother so that she reflects and responds to his needs. The infant has precisely the needs that his mother can instinctually fulfill, a form of synchronous correspondence that makes for our survival. Such mirroring installs a coherent sense of self, that is, a healthy, functional ego identity. Resourceful children whose parents were inadequate or neglectful about mirroring found their own sources of mirroring in relatives, other adults, older siblings, etc. Later in life we seek mirroring from partners in friendship and through intimate relationship.

Mirroring is unconditional positive regard shown by these five As: attention, acceptance, affection, appreciation, and allowing. Mothers and fathers gain an ability to grant these fulfilling gifts as part of becoming parents. Romantic love also makes the five As instinctive and easy to give and receive. Our self-esteem and self-respect emerge from and are sustained by a mirroring dialogue first with parents and then with those with whom we relate lovingly. Why do we fear abandonment so much? It is the withdrawal of mirroring, a necessity if we are to survive emotionally.

The opposite of the five As is shaming. This is why the more ashamed we are about ourselves, the less self-respect do we tend to have. Shame was installed where respect belonged. Shame is self-abandonment. We are wounded in ways that someday it will be our work to heal. Hopefully, we will feel compassion for the same wounds in others. This will be the synchronicity of our wounds and our compassion. In this same psychological synchronicity, self-respect is self-mirroring and leads to love in return toward those who mirror us.

Some of our feelings are felt as dangerous to others and their mirroring powers are then limited. People may, for instance, mirror our grief when our partner dies or leaves. They mirror the immediate sadness, anger, and fear that grief evokes. But a few months later, as we delve into the deeper and much more threatening depths of our grief, we may feel isolated because no one wants to go down there with us. Only very true and strong friends or therapists may be willing to be awake with us in that garden of the agony. Having them lined up for this mirroring enterprise is the synchronicity of forming friendships and relationships that will someday come through for us just as we need them to. *Who has accompanied me all the way to the bot-*

tom of the pit of myself? Have I ever thanked him / her? Have I been willing to make that trip with others?

Because of mirroring, I succeed in seeing myself through another's empathic attunement to me. This gives me a sense of validation, of effectiveness and competence and my sense of self-coherence increases. Accurate mirroring of feelings in early life—and later— leads to a comfortable body image and a strong sense of myself. A clear, cohesive, stable sense of self is thus formed by a series of mirroring experiences. Such experiences are subtle forms of synchronicity glimpsed in words like attunement, mirroring, empathy. We find what we need from those who can provide it, and that is a meaningful coincidence.

It sounds something like this: "If the original mirroring bond was lacking, I can find the missing psychic structures later in life because synchronicity will lead me to new persons who help me shore up or rebuild my own crumbling structures. This is how relationships vitalize me. The depleted is filled; the fragmented is unified; the broken is repaired. The resultant sense of mastery also increases my self-esteem and gives me a sense of continuity and power. In healthy development, I increase my capacity to internalize nurturance and it forms reliable and ineradicable structures in my psyche that replace the marred or damaged ones. The ultimate purpose and outcome of mirroring is to develop self-mirroring skills. This shows us the depth of the synchronous self-empathy that expands into compassion for others.

When we are synchronously mirrored, the circuits for our emotions are reinforced, since the brain uses the same pathways to generate an emotion as to respond to one. To reciprocate an emotion is to reinforce the capacity to feel it again—and safely, too. This is why once we are free to feel, we can feel more deeply for others. Our destiny is given a boost when we have received healthy mothering or have found a mirroring dialogue with other adults later. The bond between mother and child is the synchronicity of resource and need as are the bonds between friends.

Personal human evolution occurs in the transition from the

restricted nurturance of our original family members to a new support system of enriching people found in the wider world, a new family. A healthy person is never without such a set of ties, established through a series of synchronous meetings and relationships. Adult psychological health is not independence but interdependence, a re-satellizing of ourselves around healthy providers of mirroring. Usually, for this port to be reached, we have to embark upon our own work on ourselves first.

A person's power to fascinate or engage us may be in the perfect fit he provides for us to see where our own wounds—and/or potentialities—are. This is double synchronicity. "I may find hidden corners of my psychic house in you. I may see the deeper lineaments of my own unfaced face. Some people hit the target of who I am and of where my work is. Some hit the bull's eye and my attachment grows accordingly." A liberation happens when the other is not taken literally but as a synchronous metaphor of our own past and our deep-buried yearnings for wholeness. Others can exhume us; to is up to us to rise again.

Sometimes we feel unsupported by others. An image in nature sheds light on this condition: alder bushes grow on rocky ledges around glaciers, unsupported by soil. They fertilize themselves from air with nitrogen. Each leaf that falls in autumn richly fertilizes the ground with this nitrogen and lays the groundwork for an alder forest that will appear in the future. When our environment offers no nourishment we have to have this same skill of finding what we need from thin air. To find it is the grace of synchronicity. Emily Dickinson describes it: "Something (in us) adjusts itself to midnight." Our very identity is a synchronous cycle of seasons, a dawn following a darkness, a high tide following a low ebb, a rainbow following a storm, a getting up following a falling down. Our human enterprise has just such elegance.

I look long and honestly at my childhood and at the relationships that have been important to me throughout my life and ask myself which ones mirrored me. Is the relationship I am in now one that mirrors me? Have I and am I mirroring others and my partner? Do I show love by an unconditional acceptance, affection, attention, appreciation, and allowing the other to be herself?

I take an inventory of all my relationships: What do I appreciate in each of them? What is still unresolved? Do I owe amends to anyone? If so, I choose to make them if it seems appropriate and would not cause harm. How has each relationship shown me how to love more? How has each one opened my heart? Do I keep my heart closed now and blame it on anyone? A heart that is opening rivals in loveliness any flower that blooms.

Stories That Reveal Us and Our Relationships

Synchronicity occurs in the delicate balance between effort and aspiration. This balance is especially evident when we give up our attachment to outcomes and we notice the sudden arrival of serendipitous grace, as in this humorous story:

Maria was frustrated that at age thirty she still had not met the man of her dreams. She asked a priest for advice about how to find a suitable man to marry. "Your name tells you whom to pray to. It is Saint Joseph, spouse of Mary and patron of women who want to find a good husband." Maria bought a statue of Saint Joseph and prayed to him each morning and night for three months with no luck. Even more frustrated and now in despair, she became angry one day and threw the statue out of the window. Within a few minutes, there was a knock on her door and she opened to a man rubbing his head and holding a broken statue. This was how Maria met the man she would marry a year later. No one was surprised at the name of their first son.

There is synchronicity in how our parents met:

My mother told me how she met my father. She was in a relationship with Angelo for five years but never felt comfortable with the fact that he made his living by gambling. Mother gave him an ultimatum, either get a legitimate job or break up with her. She would not go on any more dates with him, she said, until he chose to find a new career. One night, she and her girlfriend Anna were coming out of the school where they were taking a weekly sewing class and Angelo was waiting in his car to give them both a ride home. She refused to get in the car and he followed her and Anna, slowly, stopping at every corner and pleading with them to get into the car. Anna suggested that they go to the diner nearby where her boyfriend, Ralph, a short-order cook, would soon be off work, and he would drive them home. While they were sitting in the diner having coffee, a stranger to them, but a friend of Ralph's, walked in and stared with interest at my mother. He asked Ralph to introduce him to the girl sitting with Anna. That is how my parents met and where my origins are. Our home during all my childhood was on Bradley Street. The school on Bradley and Orange streets in New Haven was my high school.

It is synchronicity when an image that has remained dormant in our imagination over the years suddenly and unexpectedly presents us with a meaning that appears at precisely the moment when it is most useful:

Here in California I have a fig tree outside my bedroom window. One morning, some years ago, in early fall, I was awakened by the ubiquitous crows that haunt my yard. They were squawking about the fact that the figs were all gone since I had picked the final fruits the day before. As I lay in bed, I suddenly remembered something from my childhood in Connecticut. At precisely this season, the Italian fathers in my neighborhood carefully, indeed tenderly, wrapped the branches of their fig trees with cloths and covered the trees with blankets and tar paper so that they could survive the harsh winter. I thought spontaneously, "If only they had shown that kind of caring to us kids!" The image of the wrapped tree had never crossed my mind until this moment, let alone this significance.

My own father, now dead, left us in Connecticut when I was two and moved to California, never to contact us again. I was the one to find my father and initiate contact when I moved west as an adult. Later that day, I suddenly remembered that it was my father who had planted the fig tree in my yard with detailed instructions about how to care for it here in California in the age-old Italian tradition.

This happened during the time that I was in therapy working on my feelings about my father. The whole event gave me so much to explore and gain from in my next therapy session. That same day that all this began, I happened to read that the Bodhi tree under which the Buddha was enlightened was a fig tree.

Synchronicity appears when a symbol that has been personally meaningful suddenly proves—or acts in accord with—its significance:

Rosalind and her fiancé chose a beautiful engagement ring for her. The large diamond symbolized the indestructible brightness of their love for each other and their commitment to a lifelong bond. On their wedding day, they confirmed this in their vows. But sadly, things did not work out as they had hoped. Four years later, they were divorced. On the day the divorce was final, Rosalind was walking from the home of her new boyfriend back to her apartment. She was on a sandy road near the beach, still wearing the ring. From the corner of her eye, she saw something bright fall to the ground. Rosalind knew instantly it was the diamond. It had suddenly fallen from its setting and sunk deep into the thick, fine sand. Rosalind looked carefully for it. Though she searched for a long time, it was nowhere or ever to be found.

Synchronicity is the essence of timing, that mysterious readiness that occurs to defy our hesitation or control. It is the moment that can become momentum:

Irene did not communicate with her sister Betty since she believed that Betty had acted unfairly regarding her mother's will. During the time of the estrangement, Irene refused all contact with Betty even though Betty had admitted her betrayal, lamented hurting her, and offered to make financial and personal amends. Irene's friends encouraged her to respond to this offer. But Irene was still feeling injured and crushed deep within. She worked on this in therapy but the release from it did not come. One day, she was walking alone along the beach when suddenly, out of nowhere, she suddenly experienced her hurt drop away and she instantaneously knew that something in her wounded ego had let go and that the time for contact had come. Irene went straight home and wrote her sister a letter, and soon they were friends again. Irene never regretted remaining true to her own timing, however, no matter what people thought of her. No one could have made her move a day earlier; no one could have stopped her a moment after.

Synchronicity can appear as a string of similar experiences that show us where we may be one-sided and where our work on ourselves may be:

Within one week, Roland ran into a great deal trouble with the women in his life. His girlfriend left him; his female boss became angry at him; his sister did not acknowledge his birthday; two women did not return his phone calls. All this happened to the man whose mother abandoned him again and again in childhood. This series of rejections/abandonments by women in such a short time threw Roland into a depression. The depression softened him and brought him into contact with his anima, that is, his feminine side. He found himself looking at and soon dealing with these issues: his abandonment of his own feminine side, his manner with women, and his fear of showing his softness. Roland made up for the lost females in his life from within himself and found his other side. This increased his appeal to women, who now found him more open and more available for intimacy.

Synchronicity is in the sudden remembrance of a personal history or series of events that reveal you to yourself or point to the next step of a path you are contemplating:

George was left by Martha on the grounds that he was not committed enough in their six-year relationship. A year later, George found himself wondering if he really was ever cut out for a live-in intimate relationship. He was ruminating about this when suddenly the whole history of his relationships flashed before him. George was astounded to realize, for the first time, that every partner of his had the same complaint that Martha had: his fear of closeness and his need for ever more space away from his partner. At the same time, he found himself admitting that intimate bonding did not quite match up with what he really wanted. The configuration of lighter relationships and deeper friendships felt more appropriate to who he was. George gradually realized that he had been following society's imposed ideal by default rather than a preferred reality by personal choice. George might now examine other areas of his life and ask, "Am I acting in accord with the reality of me or am I just doing what I always did or what everyone else does or what I am supposed to do? Does this form of relationship represent my deepest needs and wishes?" The arrival into George's mind of the two cogent pointers—his historical record and his new realization—precisely as he was facing his dilemma became the spur of the moment and was thus synchronicity.

Synchronicity appears in the fact that we choose life partners who bring up precisely the issues from our childhood past that have been waiting to be addressed so that we can lay our unfinished business to rest:

Sharon was brought up in a household with a severely abusive father. His message both explicitly and implicitly was, "You don't have what it takes to please me." No matter what she did, Sharon could never be satisfactory in her father's eyes. He belittled her efforts at pleasing him and physically and emotionally abused her throughout her stormy and unhappy childhood. To get out of the house, Sharon married at a young age. After eight years of marriage and two children, her husband Eric began having an affair with Grace, a colleague at work. Sharon was devastated by this turn of events, especially since Eric was refusing to end the affair or even to enter therapy to deal with the impact of his actions on the family. Instead, he was moving out. On the day he left, Sharon asked him what he found in Grace that he could not find in her. Eric said that she could make love the way he had always wanted it, that she could respond to his needs before he even expressed them, that she could make him feel young and desirable, and that she even kept house better than Sharon. The familiar ring to these complaints about her struck Sharon like a gong from hell. Once again, she could not please a man! Another woman could, and apparently without much effort. Her anger at Eric saved her from doing what she would have done before: try to figure out new ways to please him. Instead, Sharon went to therapy on her own and learned not to take any of this story literally. This was not about getting Eric back or hating him for what he was doing. Something much more profound was afoot. This was a repetition of her own past, a retelling of her unfinished story, an invitation to do her work on herself and get past the past. The little girl who could not please Daddy was finally getting her chance to tell her shameful tale and be done with it. Sharon became stronger over the succeeding year as she finally grieved the abuses of her woebegone past. She learned to take care of herself and to let go of the need to please men. Eric's affair was the spur for Sharon's liberation from her past and from her bondage to its frustrating and self-defeating reenactment. Grace had indeed visited Sharon and unlocked her cell door, never to be locked again by any man.

3

Our Ego and Its Coincidences

*The true Person is not an isolated entity, his individuality is
universal; for he individualizes the universe. . . .
He individualizes divine transcendence.*
—SRI AUROBINDO

Our inner life is a mystery, but there are some metaphors that can
help us understand its workings. *Ego,* the Latin word for "I," refers to
the center of our conscious rational life. The ego is functional/healthy
when it helps us fulfill our three main goals in life, that is, happiness
and serenity within ourselves, effectiveness in our tasks, and reward-
ing relationships. Our conscious rational life then becomes a resource
for sanity and happiness.

The ego becomes dysfunctional/neurotic when it distracts us
from our goals or sabotages them. Behind every neurosis is a fear or
desire that has never been addressed or resolved. *Neurotic* means
being caught in useless repetition of archaic ways of protecting ourselves against what no longer truly threatens us. We also repeat old
habits of craving that do not lead to satisfaction. This is why Jung

defines neurosis as "a defeat by the unreal." We know we are integrat-
ing ourselves effectively and are on a valid spiritual path when we become more and more functional in daily life.

The Self is the center and circumference of the entire psyche that
includes the ego. The Self is a spiritual source as the healthy ego can
be a psychological resource. This is why Jung called the Self "the God
archetype" within. The three qualities of the Self, unconditional love,
wisdom, and healing power, as outlined above, are the ones that reflect the attributes of divinity in world religions. We speak of God as
love, a Holy Spirit of wisdom, who has miraculous healing powers.
To be made in that image is to trust the presence of these gifts in us.
Our work is to release them, and thus the destiny of the Self is fulfilled through us. That destiny is the same in all beings, but each person contributes in her own individual way. Spiritual practices such as
loving-kindness are meant to assist us in acting out in our lifetime the
three eternal potentials. The ego longs to enter the service of the
Self in just those ways, if only it were not so afraid to lose its auton-
omy in the process. This is why letting go of fear is a spiritual practice.

The Self is a field of inner gravity that is sometimes unconscious
and sometimes conscious. Jung theorized that our unconscious is
both personal—containing the family album of our own memories—and cosmic—containing the mythic memories of mankind.
This collective unconscious, he said, "Contains the whole spiritual
heritage of humanity's evolution, born anew in the brain structure of
every individual."

Our ego is in us; we are in the Self. Ego is visible in our personal-
ity and bears our name. The Self is unlimited by individual personal-
ity and has no name. It is the same threefold reality in everyone:
unconditional love, eternal wisdom, and the power to heal ourselves
and others. The Self is mediated in the world by our body/ego. We
might say that the ego is our capacity for light and the Self is the light.
Once our capacity is activated, the ego becomes an incarnation of
the light of the Self.

Wisdom is not a body of truth. It is a state of being in which truth

becomes accessible within us and active through us. The big mind beyond ego looks more and more like light. As we access our powers,
our body becomes less a mule to carry us or a pedestal for our ego or
brain to rest on. Our body and all things are composed of condensed
light, continually moving, beating musically, always already united by
undying, unborn/reborn love. "Things are losing their hardness.
Even my body now lets the light through," says Virginia Woolf.

Our human enterprise, individuation, is to form or find an equi-
librium, an axis, between ego and Self. Both the ego—our conscious
life of choices—and the Self—our potential for wholeness—want
to join in this axis of wholeness. All that stands in the way is the fear
our ego has that it might lose its control and its identity, exactly what
keeps it afraid and separate. The ego/Self axis is the greatest of all coincidences because by it we unleash the powers of the Self from the
stranglehold of our frightened, limiting ego and let them flow into
the world. This is fulfillment of our human purpose. We were born
with more potential than actuality. Our task is to activate our potentials, to make them conscious, that is, articulated in our lifetime.
There is a synchronicity in this task because just as we work to activate our life purpose, an ego-Self axis, the Self moves toward us with
the same purpose. The astronomer Tim Ferris says, "Consciousness is
like a campfire in the middle of a dark Australia." Spirituality is ignit-
ing ourselves so that such a delicately wonderful thing can light up in
ourselves and in our world.

Our psychological work is to shape our ego so that it can function
without inhibition or compulsion. Then our innate gifts and talents
can enter the service of the Self and commandeer our every thought,
word, and deed into showing all the love, wisdom, and healing we
are capable of in our lifetime. The neurotic ego contravenes this
work by its prejudice that we are separate, in control, and in no need
of humility. The *Course in Miracles* says, "Your choice to use this device
[ego] *enables* it to endure." Our psychological work is to dismantle
our neurotic ego in favor of our functional ego. As we saw above, our
ego is functional when it guides us on our path. If I want to go north,
my body is functional when I walk in a northerly direction. If I walk

south to go north, something has become dysfunctional, that is, neurotic, based on illusion. The functional ego is the best vehicle for the emergence of the Self, yet, by grace, the neurotic ego too can be harnessed.

Saint John of the Cross wrote, "Swiftly, with nothing spared, I am being completely dismantled." Nothing less is required for spiritual growth than the total dissolution of the inflated ego. Half measures do not avail. Inflation is the habit of imagining and acting as if the whole purpose of life was one's own aggrandizement and the fulfillment of one's own entitlements. This means bringing attention only to our own needs, demanding to be in control, believing we are entitled to be served by everyone and to have the ordinary conditions of existence repealed or relaxed for us because we are so special. Joseph Campbell says, "Hell is being stuck in ego." He is referring to the neurotic ego with its compulsive attachment to fear and grasping. Intimate relationships help most in the dismantling of the illusions of our controlling and entitled egos. They show up the ego's entitlements as fictions that fade in the face of loving-kindness toward all.

The neurotic side of the ego is not meant to be destroyed but, paradoxically, to be expanded in its healthy humility so that it can extend its creative possibilities to all our psyche. It is liberated by being relieved of its arrogance and then opened to its potential to show power *for* rather than power *over* others. This is also our potential for bringing peace into the world and into our relationships. A hero is a person who lives through the pain of this process and is thereby transformed by it. Such a transformation reveals us to ourselves as singular and as one with all that is: "All the lotus lands and all the Buddhas are revealed in my own being," says the *Avatamsaka Sutra*.

Our psyche is driven by a spontaneous urge toward wholeness and therefore strives to harmonize apparent polarities: conscious and unconscious, ego and Self. It is up to us to further this process or to let it slumber. Our lively aspiration might be, "I feel a homing instinct for wholeness. I do what it takes to break the spell of ego."

Our functional ego adapts to the external world by socialized behavior and extroversion (mediated by our persona, the appearance we present to others). It adapts to the internal world by introversion (mediated by our shadow, the dark side of us that we hide from others and from ourselves). Our ego becomes more and more functional by disidentifying with any exclusive attachment to our persona, by reclaiming our shadow projections, and by recovering our body as a legitimate and useful tool in the adventure of living.

The shadow is the part of us that is hidden and unconscious to us. Our negative shadow contains all that we find unacceptable about ourselves but disavow. We then strongly detest in ourselves what we cannot see in ourselves. Our positive shadow holds our untapped potential. We admire in others what is buried and deactivated in us. Synchronicity, meaningful coincidence, happens as we meet up with just the people who activate our positive shadow gifts and our negative shadow traits. Both strong dislike and admiration are the projections we can reclaim, and they are synchronously just what we require for a sense of wholeness.

Healthy ego:	*Spiritual Self:*
Resources:	The source:
Observe	Unconditional love
Assess	Perennial wisdom
Act in accord with goals	Healing power
Make choices that reflect our deepest wishes and needs	

The work is to return to the source through the healthy ego's resources. The source is within. It is the Self beyond the clinging ego, an enlightened nature perfect in essence but imperfectly exhibited in daily existence. I can find a perfect bee but not a perfect me. A bee is perfect without effort. I have to work at being who and all that I already am.

PRACTICING LETTING GO OF EGO

Spiritual awakening involves maintaining a healthy ego and letting go of the inflated—neurotic—ego with such central themes as those listed below. Notice which ones apply to you:

> I become enraged, spiteful, and vindictive when I am thwarted, found to be in error, or bested (even in board games or sports)
>
> I have to win, cannot be second, and will not be last
>
> I have to be right, noticed, and praised
>
> I overreact to minor slights
>
> I hold a grudge when crossed and have to get even
>
> I will not forgive or forget
>
> I insist on getting my own way most of the time
>
> I find flexibility or compromise difficult
>
> I am controlling, demanding, manipulative
>
> I am abusive, sarcastic, territorial, possessive
>
> I operate on a hierarchical (not cooperative) dominance model
>
> I demand that I be highly appreciated for every good deed
>
> I have to be excused for every misdeed, denying or justifying my misbehavior and canceling any need for amends
>
> I cannot be criticized or even given feedback without becoming defensive or aggressive
>
> I cannot lose face, that is, lose ego, nor can I apologize
>
> I have to come out looking good
>
> I believe I am entitled to an exemption from the conditions of ordinary existence
>
> I demand love, respect, and loyalty no matter what
>
> I have to return a favor (keep it even, don't be beholden to anyone)
>
> I cannot show that I need others or that I am dependent on them in any way
>
> Retaliation is my favorite sport

Note the compulsive, aggressive—and painful—flavor of all the above. The lifestyle of the inflated ego is compulsive since we *have* to act in these ways, lest we lose control or the rank we believe ourselves entitled to, even at any cost of our own peace of mind. In fact, there is no peace when ego rules. It is aggressive because of its "me first" attitude and its retaliatory, punitive flavor. It is painful because the person with this neurotic ego is full of fear, feels terribly anxious about losing face, and notices that, though he may win, he certainly is not being loved. In a job in which he has even minimal authority, he may demand rigid adherence to the rules, lord it over others, and strongly punish those who defy his authority.

Ask yourself: Does my ego become confused with self-reliance?

"I won't give up (or in)."

"I keep my word."

"I said I'll do it and I will."

These may be self-reliance *or* ego. They are examples of self-reliance when they are flexible and interdependent in how they play out. They are ego when they are unilateral, self-centered, and meant to establish and maintain an arrogant persona. How do they size up in my life?

An example of the capacity of the ego to sustain its rage and indignation is in the instance of the divorced man who kidnaps his children and keeps them away from their mother for years. Another might be in someone who refuses to talk to a friend for years after a single instance of being snubbed. One affront, even unintended, can keep the ego angry and mean-spirited for the rest of one's life. The essence of the neurotic ego is the terror of having to face the conditions of existence without control over them or entitlement to exemption from them. In healthy relating, our ego-control is deposed in favor of equality. Entitlement becomes asking for what we want with the understanding that we may not get it. Our indignation (ego anger) then shows itself as sadness about not being loved as we wanted to be and, paradoxically, we become much more lovable.

Here are some declarations that help alter the ego's compulsions.

You can use them as aspirations, and they become a part of your spiritual practice:

> I give up having to get my way.
> I let go of controlling and manipulating others.
> I am open to appreciation, understanding, and love and let go of demanding it.
> I admit when I am wrong and make amends.
> I invite others to call me on my mistakes.
> I accept the fact that I do not always win or gain.
> I ask for what I want without demanding it, and I can take no for an answer.
> I am fully responsible for my behavior and predicament.
> I love, respect, and make allowances for others.
> I forego the wish or plan to punish or hurt others.
> I forego the desire and plan to retaliate.
> I am becoming truer to my higher Self, where unconditional love abounds.
> As I let my ego urges be dissolved, I discover and uncover my indestructible Self.

Note the generous sweetness of all the above! Show this practice section to three people: your significant other or best friend, the person who criticizes you the most, and a member of your family of origin. Ask each of them to suggest which listings seem to apply to you. Thank each of them without putting up any argument. Humility without humiliation is the best path to letting go of the arrogant ego.

LOSING/SAVING FACE

The ego is inflated when its main concern is saving F. A. C. E.: **f**ear, **a**ttachment, **c**ontrol, and **e**ntitlement. The ego does not know its first name, fear, only its last name, entitlement. To be caught in the rigidities of the arrogant ego is to live in fear. Transformation is letting love no longer be only a letting in but also a letting through. This can happen because love was behind our fear all the while, waiting for its chance to scale the wall and then to sift through us to everyone else. We provide the Self that chance when we let go of ego. This is what is meant by saying that spirituality and compassion begin with the dismantling of ego. Wisdom/compassion means that we have finally seen through our habit of self-positioning and self-aggrandizement. Once we see how much of our creative energy we sink into saving F. A. C. E., we notice so many others doing the same useless thing and compassion happens.

It seems that it is healthy not to care too much about others' opinions of us. To say that others' opinions and reactions to us do not matter does not mean that others do not matter. It is only to say that we have an immovable center of great value, and that no one can supplant it or is needed to enhance it. Freedom from fear and craving protects the soul's core with healthy boundaries. A healthy ego sets these boundaries and maintains them.

It follows from all this that people and events that challenge and deflate our ego are assisting forces on our journey to the greatest of all synchronicities in human fulfillment, the ego/Self axis, our life purpose. Each assisting force that comes along in meaningful coincidences is a personification of grace. Ego enemies are friends of the Self. We might say it this way: "The woman who betrayed me, the boss who fired me, the son who turned against me, the friend who called me on my selfishness, the teacher who showed me how much I needed to learn may all have been players in the touching drama of my uphill liberation from ego. Each helped me by giving me the opportunity to let go of my arrogant entitlements in favor of humility and vulnerability, the antechambers to the throne-room of love, the real power in my life. The fact that just the right people appeared at just the right time in just the right place is a dazzling synchronicity."

The afflicting forces in our story were the fear-driven people and institutions that imposed the shoulds and rigid restrictions that were self-limiting, not self-protecting. They were *guards against* our freedom. The assisting forces were those who provided flexibility and liberty to experience and experiment. They were the *guardians of* our freedom. Who comes to mind and what were the synchronous events that brought us together?

Spiritual warrior energy applied to the dismantling of ego takes two forms: taking hold and letting go/letting be. The warrior's work is accomplished by self-discipline, ultimately a form of healthy self-love. Self-denial—ego denial—is "not denial of me but of the me that gets in the way," says W. H. Auden. The spiritual warrior's work is also done by simply sitting, letting be. Synchronicity lets us know just when to hold on or let go: a series of losses invites us to let go; a series of opportunities encourages us to take hold. A bear knows when to fight and claw her way to what she wants and when to lie down and let nature take its somnolent course. She does by natural instinct what we do by spiritual attentiveness to synchronicity. Look at the metaphor of hibernation. The bear enters a self-dug cave for one to four months with no eating or drinking since he survives on his own body fat, even recycling his own waste. He awakes weighing 25 percent less than he weighed when he lay down. Can I let that much of my ego go? Instead, will I want to stay on guard and in full control and refuse to lie down, ever?

The Tibetan teacher Chögyam Trungpa taught that there is something sane and awake in us that is shut off when we are struggling through our dramas and holding our ego position in them. This something sane and awake is the transcendent function of the psyche that always comes up with a healing alternative in the form of an image or path that cuts through our dilemmas, no matter how confounding. It comforts us and shows us our inner resources. It comes to life in the gaps between our struggles. We stop to take time out and sit in what is. This is how Buddha sat. We often overvalue the consensual point of view that confirms our ego habits, and we thereby automatically reject these gaps or refuse to see them at all. Liberating moments hap-

pen when a habitual pattern is interrupted in favor of something altogether new, a gap in the ego's same old story.

The humbling journey through ego is addressed paradoxically in
the *Tao Te Ching*: "Attain the climax of emptiness." When we assent to
emptying ourselves of ego, Taoists say that we stumble upon a "mysterious pass through the apparently impenetrable mountains." It
opens in the midst of the jagged rocks. It appears where thoughts,
fantasies, fears, and desires cease. It is the pause between stimulus
and response, just where freedom resides. It is the pause between
our dramatic storylines. There we become the fair and alert witnesses, and a serene sanity arises in us. This pause/pass is the soul
space between ego and Self. It is the heart of us and the soul of the
universe, now finally acknowledged as one and the same. In other
words, it is the point at which we become and are synchronicity.
"After the Way is realized, there is nowhere that is not the mysterious
pass," says the Taoist Ho Yang.

The road is fraught with danger because we are involved in a rite
of passage from outside ego/persona to inside Self, from the periph-
ery to the center of the mandala of wholeness, from the profane to
the sacred, from the ephemeral to the eternal, from the mortal to
the immortal, from the divided to the united. Immortality refers to
a state beyond the limits of ego and the conditions of our existence.
Attaining this center requires the equivalent of ego death. It is a consecration to and initiation into the sacred, that is, the discovery of
one's spirituality. It is the ultimate answer to the question, Why am I
here? I am here to live out my destiny "on earth as it is in heaven."
This sounds trite at first but look more closely:

"On earth" is the metaphor for our psychological work of build-
ing a healthy ego, one that will be an apt instrument for our spiritual
work. "In heaven" is the metaphor for the spiritual work of releasing
unconditional love, universal wisdom, and healing power into the
world. Now look at the three little words that are the bridge between: "As it is." When I say Yes to the "as it is," I create the bridge between earth and heaven, between my psychological and spiritual
work, between my ego mortality and my immortal destiny.

EGO/SELF AT A GLANCE

The Self is the core of our very being. We use a capital "S" to distinguish this archetypal Self, an ancient collective energy in the psyche, from the self in lowercase, which refers to the ego or persona.

Our Self is essential, that which is permanent and indestructible in us.

Ego is existential, changing in accord with the demands, fears, or desires of the moment. It takes the form of action.

Our destiny is to exhibit existentially what is in us essentially. This is letting the light of the Self through the wounds and openings of the ego into the world. Our work is to display in our ego actions and choices the eternal design of the Self: love, wisdom, healing. This incarnational project is what is meant by "an axis of ego and Self."

There is essential synchronicity in this aptitude for axis (individuation) in our psyche. Existential synchronicity appears in the moment that initiates or furthers the axis work. Essential synchronicity is in the eternal harmony of ego/Self and soul/universe. This is the harmony we discover in meditation. Existential synchronicity is in the meaningful coincidences that point our ego to its path. It is something we notice in our conscious attention to our life process.

MAKING EGO-FREE CHOICES

Synchronicity's messages become louder as they are listened to—as more letters are more likely from a person who knows we are reading them and responding to them seriously. Psychic literacy is the ability to read these messages; spirituality is the choice to respond to them. How do the messages come to us? They may come in synchronicity, dreams, intuitions, projection, psychic phenomena and readings, inner guides, events beyond our control, visions, sudden spontaneous powers, déjà vu, religious or mystical realizations, meditation/contemplation, an impetus from art or beauty, or active imagination.

Spiritual choices are those in which we hearken to and say Yes to these messages. To say Yes is to let the Self take precedence over ego. The F.A.C.E. of ego changes: Fear becomes love. Attachment becomes letting go. Control becomes allowing and honoring others' freedom. Entitlement becomes standing up for our rights without retaliation if they are not respected. These transformations make us unconditionally loving, wise, and a source of healing, the qualities of the Self.

Thus, a spiritual choice has two main characteristics. It expresses unconditional/universal love, perennial wisdom, and healing power, and it emanates from an unconditional *yes* to the conditions of existence. It includes an awareness of and a trust in the friendliness of psyche and matter. Since the transcendent has entered the temporal, consciousness is indivisible. Material events and tangible realities declare the conditions of cosmic consciousness.

A spiritual choice is one that honors inner rhythms that may not match conventional milestone choices: "There are waves by which a life is marked, a rounding off that has nothing to do with events," wrote Virginia Woolf in her journal. Awareness of our personal spiritual messages helps us ride the waves rather than be drowned by them (overincorporate stimuli from outside) or run from them (underincorporate outside stimuli). *What in me has remained steadfastly meaningful through all the vicissitudes of my life? That is what has nurtured me.*

How can one know which messages are from the inner Self and which are merely fictions of the ego? First, true messages feel so strong and real, they feel as if they could not be otherwise. One has a felt sense, an intuitive certainty that they are authentic. Secondly, authentic messages arrive along more than one avenue, for example, not only in synchronicity but also in dreams and intuitions, etc. Thirdly, a true message does not submit to the ego's attempts to dismiss it. Finally, authentic messages move us in the direction of love, wisdom, and healing. They are never aimed at boosting the self-serv-ing ends of the ego.

If our choice is to have recourse to astrology or other divination modalities, do we seek wisdom about our spiritual path or advice about how which investment to choose? The oracle of Apollo at Del-phi was closed in Christian times. It had fallen into misuse and had lost its numinous power. People were asking ego questions—how to have more—rather than how to go beyond desire to destiny. There was no room left for miraculous wisdom, and so it passed away with-out protest when the emperor discontinued it. Oracular wisdom may be demolished in us once ego ambition crushes the spirit of a transcendent intent.

Appropriate spiritual choices find a resonance in nature. Plato says, "The motions akin to the divine part of us are the orbits of the universe. Everyone may follow these, correcting those circuits in the brain that were deranged at birth. We need to learn the harmonies of the universe." The poet Baudelaire adds, "Man walks through forests of physical things that are also spiritual things and they watch him af-fectionately." To learn from nature makes sense since we are part of her and children resemble their mother. To allow seasons of bloom-ing and decay, to welcome changing conditions and patterns, to hi-bernate in some seasons and activate in others, to live and be ready to die, these are nature's lessons and lesions. To acknowledge their applicability to ourselves is to join in their celebratory cycles of re-newal. This is conscious alignment to the synchronicity of nature. Our interpretation is correct when it leads to "Yes!"

This sign I once saw at Patrick's Point in Humboldt, California, strikes a chord here: "Relentlessly, wave swells roll in toward the shallows, rise high, break into foaming crests, and plunge onto the shore. Waves are born when winds create friction with the sea's sur-face and infuse it with energy. As waves near the shore, the rising slope of the bottom of the ocean forces them into crests, and then into breakers. Waves release enormous energy when they crash upon the shore. All life in the surf zone must be able either to hide or to hold on for dear life."

JUST COINCIDENCE

The Trickster Ego

> A greater power than we can contradict hath thwarted
> our intents.
>
> —WILLIAM SHAKESPEARE, *Romeo and Juliet*

In *Tom and Jerry* cartoons, Jerry, the powerless mouse, overcomes and outwits Tom, the powerful cat. The humor is in the reversal of nature's usual arrangement. We see this reversal also in *The Wizard of Oz*: little Dorothy kills the powerful witch. In the Christmas mystery, a helpless infant intimidates the powerful King Herod. Lowly characters continually humble imperious ones. The trickster is the archetype of that comeuppance. We have certainly noticed in our own lives how persons and events keep coming along to depose our ego's arrogance, to show us how little in control we really are, to strip us of our imaginary entitlements, to disrupt our best laid schemes. Such people and events are trickster visits to us, more assisting forces on our path.

The trickster is the ego demolitions expert who helps us become more realistic about our psychological limitations and ultimately our spiritual limitlessness. He leads us to border crossings where we are tricked into finding our own wholeness. This is an energy within ourselves and within the universe that humbles us, topples our ego, upsets our plans, demonstrates to us how little our wishes matter, and dissolves the forms that no longer serve us though we may be clinging to them for dear life. Comfort and routine are the two sworn enemies of our lively energy, and the trickster battles these enemies on our behalf. His visits may feel like plagues, but they are gifts in the long run.

The trickster is the mythic personification of synchronicity. Within all of us is an instinct to consolidate an axis between ego and Self. To do this requires some deflating of our ego. The trickster is the archetype of that deflation. The trickster in relationship is that man who fooled you, that woman who betrayed you, that predator/

partner who used you, that shyster who took your money, etc. In each instance, someone, something, or some event turned your life upside down or showed you how vulnerable you were, how you were not all you cracked yourself up to be. Fear and desire are the calisthenics of the trickster ego, and the rough tools he uses to show the ego its inadequacy.

Humor, irony, and paradox are the milder transformative tools of the trickster, the transpersonal source of wit. A pretty face may be the trickster; alcohol and cocaine are the trickster; romantic attachment is the trickster; the penis is definitely a trickster. All of these can absorb our energy, direct our choices, fool us into mistakes, and lead us to desperate addiction and out-of-control behavior. We are seduced into believing that any of these can grant us permanent happiness or increase our personal stature. Indeed, the trickster makes the same promises that Adam and Eve fell prey to when this whole human enterprise began.

The trickster is the archetype of synchronicity and of illusion and ambiguity. He tricks us out of the status quo and into new perspectives through unruly events that at first seem negative but become positive or at first seem positive and then show themselves to be negative. The trickster archetype is the psyche's answer to oppression and grandiosity. Fearless and uncompromising, it exposes pretension and pomposity wherever we manifest it or fall prey to it. The joker or fool fulfilled this function for the king in medieval courts. The king chose to be in the company of the trickster; we meet him unawares, unready, and unsuspecting.

Opposites constellate in the psyche as complementaries. This is because the psyche reconciles while the ego attempts to divide. We all contain both arrogance and humility. An inner force of Self wants to reconcile these polarities. When we are overly arrogant, the trickster may humble us. He makes our hidden humility conscious and visible. Then our arrogance becomes tamed and appears as healthy self-esteem. This is how opposites are reconciled as complementaries. The trickster fosters such wholeness in spite of our ego's objections or resistance. He will not allow one-sidedness but will arrange our circumstances so that our other side will have its chance to emerge. Selfish people may be forced by a crisis to be selfless; macho men may be forced to be tender. Big shots may be forced to knuckle under. Indeed, wholeness, the opposite of one-sidedness, often comes into our lives uninvited. The trickster is its escort, cruel in order to be kind.

The trickster character in stories dupes and is duped, gets into trouble and out of it too, shuffles chance and mischance, shows the hero his dark side, has irresistible charm, is spontaneous and unpredictable. He is a comic or a jinx who employs art, artifice, sedition, and dishonesty. The trickster energy appears in unexpectedness, mischief, disorder, shock, or amorality. He balances rigid and righteous attitudes with humor and flexibility. He comes to the entrenched to release spontaneity and thus restore psychic balance, thwarts careful plans, creates inner and outer upheavals, induces or forces us into new arrangements, topples thrones and supplants the royal ego. He is the lord of topsy-turvy, the hand that pushed Humpty Dumpty to his great fall.

The trickster helps deflate the warrior version of heroism in which the object is only to triumph over an opponent rather than to win over an opponent by honor, honesty, and love. The trickster leads us to a primordial dawn of order from dissonance. He devours ego, unites opposites, and thereby transforms meaninglessness into meaningfulness, predicament into path, sterile voids into fertile pastures, stuckness into a way out, and ultimately, death into life.

In our culture, the trickster has appeared as the Cheshire cat, Bugs Bunny, Daffy Duck, the Road Runner, etc. The trickster is Puck, Ariel, poltergeists, the Joker, the devil, imps, sprites. He is a rascal and a prankster but not totally a scoundrel. These are all personifications of an energy in us and in the world of synchronicity that we encounter in daily life.

The trickster is the oldest of all mythic characters, hence the Crow and Blackfoot see him as the Old Man. His longevity is explained by the liveliness of the stories about him and our fascination with them: "So stubborn a refusal to forget could not be an accident," says the anthropologist Paul Radin, referring to the trickster. In other native cultures, he is a rabbit, raven, coyote, spider, monkey, and plumed serpent. He is the clever animal who helps in time of need and upsets the plans of those who think they have no needs. He comes from and leads us into a realm in which the controlling ego is exposed as the great pretender and a more realistic self assumes its rightful power.

In Greek mythology, some heroes and gods become tricksters. Dionysus is the trickster when he grants greedy Midas's wish. Eris, the goddess of strife, is the trickster who triggers the Trojan War with her golden apple. Hermes the trickster is the principal god of synchronicity. He meets us with lucky chances and windfalls. As a god of ambiguity, he invented language that explains *and* hides, hence his name gives us the words *hermeneutics* and *hermetic*. Hermes is the messenger, the god mediating between the ego world and the world of the Self. He is the God of revelation who manifests spirit in matter, showing how matter matters, the god of alchemy cooking up the precious from the useless.

Since he was born at night in a cave, Hermes can see at night, that is, he can see our shadow and force us to see it and thereby show us how to learn from it. Zeus gave him the task/gift of bringing souls to Hades and back again. He is thus the mediator who bridges the gap between life and death. It was he who brought Persephone back from the underworld. Hermes is the *psychopomp,* the guide of souls, who guides us to the ego-slaying underworld, our own unconscious. Hermes is indeed the personification of the unconscious, of prime matter, and of the power to hold all opposites, both material and spiritual. Thus the trickster energy is the artificer of our individuation—the consummation of personal wholeness. So much of our destiny is in humorous hands.

Hermes was invoked as the patron god of the crossroads. The ancients believed that choices of paths took more than the human ego to navigate. Transcendent help was required and was gladly bestowed by Hermes, especially through synchronicities, but often in tricky ways. The cover of this book shows the road sign that is sometimes used to alert drivers to crossings on the road ahead. The trickster energy meets us at crossings, a metaphorical description of synchronicity. In the course of life we are wise to be ready for many unexpected characters crossing our path. To believe that our ego provides all the support we need in those moments might be the most comical of all our human notions. To trust that grace wants to come our way may rouse a cosmic smile upon us.

PRACTICING AN ETIQUETTE FOR TRICKSTER VISITS

> He has pulled down the mighty from their thrones; he has exalted the lowly.
>
> —LUKE 1:52

In each of the following listings, try to locate the positive and negative hidden parts of yourself or of the events and people that have influenced you.

- A treasure is lost or found: I have powers or riches but am tricked out of them by promises or misplaced trust and thereby lose them, for example, the young man who leaves his gold in the keeping of the dishonest innkeeper.
- I am humiliated by being bested by someone I thought was less than myself in skill or intelligence, for example, the tortoise and hare story or my showing off at bat and then being struck out by a rookie pitcher.
- I am planning to quit in a huff when I am fired.
- I am shown to be quite fragile by my overreaction to a practical joke.
- I am shocked to realize my partner is using the time I am off having an affair to have one herself.
- I think I am really loved by someone who wants only my money.

- I am head over heels in love with someone and many synchronicities occur that seem to point to my having found
my soul mate, yet it all proves to be an illusion.
- While engaged to be married, I fall head over heels in love
with someone who does not reciprocate. The whole experience shows me how little in love I was with my fiancée.
- A visit from the trickster happens most often through personal crisis. This corresponds to the dismemberment experience of the hero, that is, the dismantling of ego. We are
broken up, we are forced to let go. The hero descends to
the underworld to converse with sages and shamans and
then ascends to converse with gods. Through such symbolic death we are all likely to be reborn. The whole event
is like the rope trick in which the body ascends, falls to the
ground in pieces, and is reassembled. But we remember
what Pliny said when he saw the colossus of Rhodes in broken pieces on the ground after an earthquake, "Even in
pieces it was a wonder of the world!"

Identify in the list of trickster visits above the ones that have happened to you and how you handled them. How do they entrench or
release you? How would humor have changed your experience of
trickster visits? Who are the people or events or circumstances in
your life who have served as tricksters? How have you been a trickster to others?

If you feel that you are willing to work with trickster energy, try
the following:

- Notice the humor in what you are feeling or sensing in any
here and now
- Say Yes to what is, like it or not
- Allow things to remain topsy-turvy for a day longer than
you can stand
- Don't look for soft landings but allow yourself to land on
concrete reality
- Learn from the surprises that come your way

- Welcome crisis as ego deflation, that is, your coziness has been addressed, processed, and resolved by the universe
- Invite the pain of change rather than avoiding it
- Have less self-importance
- Find a way of "playing with pain," what Charlie Chaplin called the secret of his humor
- Invent rituals that take you out of character—as happens at costume parties or on Halloween, Mardi Gras, or April Fool's Day
- Most of our daily routine is habit rather than creative design. Try forsaking your routine some day in order to be totally open to what might happen.
- Go out of character. Explore very different lifestyles or belief systems, try entirely new interests or careers, change personal habits and choices even briefly from fear-based to courage-based, from tight to loose, from inhibited to experimental, from *no* to *yes*.

We don't have to struggle to be free. Absence of struggle is freedom.

—CHÖGYAM TRUNGPA

4

Our Time and Place

ONLY ONE WORLD

*The difference between the cosmos and man is only one of degree
not essence. . . . Nature expresses something which transcends it. . . .
The display (what we see) is dual but the reality is identical. . . .
The reality of matter is the psychic self.*
—MIRCEA ELIADE

The fact that meaningful coincidences happen to us beyond our
conjuring gives us evidence that we are not alone in the world.
Rather, the world is wonderfully in on the fulfillment of our own life
purpose. The most brilliant fact that synchronicity reveals is the oneness of the world and our inner selves. The psyche and the world are,
in effect, two aspects of one actuality. The universe shows an intuitive, coherent, caring directedness. This creative ordering principle
is revealed in synchronicity. It is as if life itself wants us to actualize
and is orchestrating events that foster it. That is the equivalent of a
loving intent. My role as a free being is to say Yes to the love that my
ego is afraid of but that the Self is made of.

What John Muir said of nature applies to us too: "When we try to pick out anything by itself, we find it is hitched to everything else in the universe." We live in a natural orbit that is likewise unlimited in its interconnectedness. Quantum theory in modern physics acknowledges and confirms this when it sees particles not as mass but as interconnections: the relatedness of things *are* things. How significant that Saint Thomas Aquinas's simplest definition of spirituality was "an interconnectedness with all things."

The fully extended psyche thus includes the "external world." Jung stated it this way: "The psyche is not localized in space. . . . The psyche is not in us; we are in the psyche. . . . The soul is mostly outside the body. . . . Psyche and body are not separate entities but one and the same life. . . . Ultimately, every individual life is the same as the eternal life of the species." This is a way of saying that there is something in us that transcends us. It is the same something that beckons to us from nature. It is the call of the wild to spiritual wholeness. Indeed, the Self calls the ego through nature. The inner world of the ego and the outer world of nature are facets of the cosmic Self. The sixteenth-century alchemist Sendivogius commented, "The greater part of the soul lies outside the body." Our mind is not in our cranium any more than a newscaster is in our television. The brain is only the most local region of mind. In that realization, we see again how our own soul work is indeed world work. "The soul *is* the universe!" wrote Meister Eckhart.

In medieval times, the phrase *unus mundus,* "one world," referred to the unity of matter and spirit ever communicating and interacting. Joseph Campbell beautifully sums up the implication: "The hero and his god . . . are the outside and inside of a single self-mirrored mystery, which is identical with the mystery of the manifest world." The psyche and the universe is a hologram: all of everything is in every part of it all. Every cell in us is a hologram of the universe. All existence is a continuum of continuous creation that moves, dances in rhythmic progress. The cosmos found a way to become conscious. *I am that way.*

Synchronicity is an affidavit that there is an *unus mundus,* a single reality with many locales. No dualism means opposites are relative, not independent. Nothing is mutually exclusive. Reality is not composed of wholes or parts but whole-parts. Marsilio Ficino, a Renaissance Florentine philosopher, saw the universe as one living being with the cosmos as its body and the psyche as its soul. Synchronicity transcends and contains both psyche and matter since synchronicities are special moments in which the unity of psyche and matter becomes manifest. Every synchronicity is an epiphany of this unity. Every synchronicity presents a death warrant to dualism.

The physicist David Bohm sees the universe as an indivisible whole and the observable world as an unfolded "explicate" order of an underlying enfolded "implicate" order. Both coexist hologrammatically, that is, every part contains the whole. Matter and consciousness both have explicate (manifest) order and underlying implicate (hidden) order. "What is" is actually a psycho-physical unity behind which is a "vast sea of energy" that is unfolding in space and time. Synchronicity is also described in this same way, and so is everything about us.

Our body is not limited to the physical but extends in the universe—which is itself our larger body, a mystical body. Ecology is thus not about our taking care of nature as an object but as an extension of our own being. Our body, physically, is one of the limited planes on which spiritual events can happen. Our body, hologrammatically, is not limited material but unlimited wholeness.

To be afraid of the ongoing tides of change is, in this context, not trusting the *unus mundus,* the oneness of the world of nature with our inner world. Nature can be looked to as an assisting force in our destiny. Nature transforms death to life and continually promotes the union of opposites. This same synthesis happens in dreams and in synchronicity. In both, conscious and unconscious reveal our one life-affirming inclination toward Self-actualization. Grasping gets in the way of our seeing this because we grasp for something we believe we need that is outside us. That perpetuates our illusion of an "out there," the opposite of the *unus mundus.*

As we saw above, there is something about us that is independent of our personal story, that is, something collectively shared and innate, archetypal. The archetypes are psychoid; they contain both psyche and matter. Archetypes are innate patterns and themes in the human psyche, the same the world over. These "primordial images," as Jung calls them, make up humanity's collective unconscious. They are the vehicles to understanding and handling life's deepest realities: love, death, sex, aggression, religious experience, etc. These archetypal themes are not separate but continually interactive. Thus, when one of these archetypes becomes activated in us by a powerfully charged external event or transition, then similar—synchronous—events gather around us. It is as if they want to become openings into meaning and completion. Now we see how synchronicity originates, how it combines inner and outer worlds, and how it leads to meaning and fulfillment.

Synchronicity confirms the unity of outside/inside as aspects rather than separate entities. This is another confirmation that our dreams, ancient myths, and the perennial—archetypal—philosophy all say the same thing: "In the ever-present light of no-boundary awareness, what we once imagined to be the isolated self in here turns out to be all of a piece with the cosmos out there," says Ken Wilber in *No Boundary*. Everything is synchronicity because everything is everything.

Lucien Lévi-Bruhl, the French anthropologist, originated a phrase to show the unconscious identification of mankind and the world: *participation mystique*. This primal fusion was symbolized in primitive times by a totem (guardian) ancestral animal. The mature belief in the one-with-all comes to mean that the divisive ego has been deposed and that materiality and spirit are aspects of the same unitary reality.

The reality of the phenomenal world is an ongoing tide of transformation with which we learn to flow. A fixation on Apollonian order creates an obstacle to this Dionysian realization with its uncontrollable and surprising challenges. For the ancient Greeks, the world would not survive if the Eleusinian mysteries (death/resurrection rites) were not enacted. This is another way of saying that our individual work and cosmic work are interdependent and one. Indeed, the archetype of the *unus mundus* is the Self since both denote wholeness and unity. It is the unity of Self and world that was divided by the ego's pomp and circumstance, proclaiming itself to be all there is. Recovered unity is thus what is really meant by "higher consciousness." The ego enlists itself with alacrity into the service of the Self.

The unity is expressed tenderly in a sermon by the early Christian theologian Origen: "You have within yourself the herds of cattle, flocks of sheep, and the fowls of the air. You are a world in miniature with a sun, a moon, and many stars." Nature is thus a theophany, an epiphany of the divine Self. Our body/ego is part of nature, not its opponent. The balance of nature is itself synchronicity. There is even another and more profound level of synchronicity in nature: its particular beauty on this planet is the only level of beauty that can satisfy such sophisticated beings as ourselves. Only this precise quality of nature can match the aesthetic sense that we were born with.

An animal is equipped with a range of behaviors apposite to his environment. When a stimulus is presented, an innate automatic mechanism swings into action and an appropriate response is released. He acts in the best interest of his—and all of nature's—survival. In the same way, we inherit archetypal predispositions that endow us with all we need to flourish in our physical, emotional, and spiritual environment. They are like adaptive equipment in our psyche to help us respond to events and conditions of life in a way that shines in as a fulfillment of destiny. It is astonishing to realize that the equipment of nature and of the psyche are synchronously one: homeostasis, regulated growth, self-restoration, and cyclic renewal, all geared to balance in nature's ecology and in our psyche.

It now seems clear that synchronicity is the meeting point of the two realms we see as matter and psyche. The world archetype is united to the Self archetype with the conscious ego as their bridge. Synchronicity is the symbol and manifestation of the ultimate oneness of what appears within us as an inner world of the psyche and what appears before us as the outer world of matter. It is the parapsychological equivalent of the *unus mundus*—as a mandala is its inner psychic equivalent. In both of these the psychic and the physical are one coin with two sides. One value remains and divisions disappear.

Taoism is a Chinese philosophical system that recommends a respect for synchronicity. The Tao is the harmony of the universe, and to act in accord with it is happiness as well as sanity. Tao equates reality with the natural law governing all life and lifetimes. In the Hindu and Buddhist traditions, dharma is the moral law that upholds the universe. These Eastern views are ways of acknowledging the meaningful interconnectedness of all things. Our destiny is to make and carry through the decisions that support and synchronize with the reliable order of Tao and dharma—always and already in progress. Tao grants primacy to a force beyond the ego that does not impose order but exposes it. This is the synchronicity of time, people, and events that come to meet us and to show us our destiny. To honor the Tao is to commit ourselves to the unfolding story by cooperation with these cooperators. Since psyche and universe are one reality, the same Tao that works personally with us is also the invisible works, the working order of the world. Something in us is enthusiastically geared to harmonize with that order and rhythm. It is not a logical decision in our brain but a musical disposition in our soul. True work on ourselves flows from and with this rhythmic urge toward wholeness, a rumba within and around us.

> A pure space appears before us where flowers ceaselessly open.
>
> —RAINER MARIA RILKE

THE TIME IT TAKES

Life, to be perfect, must be possessed altogether: there must be no past which is gone, no present which is going, no future which is to come. It must be permanent, abiding, full, and without succession. Life which would be past is lost life;

that which is to come would not be life possessed; and that
which is passing is life in decay.

—EDWARD LEEN

The world of places is one with our inner world in this moment
in time. Are we living exclusively in time-bound awareness or in
unity consciousness in which time and eternity are one? Synchronicity plays out its pattern across the boundaries of time, since time and
timelessness are two sides of a single coin in the realm of the Self. We
are carefully tied to nature and history but only occasionally get a
glimpse of this wonderful simultaneity.

Historic time is linear following the calendar without repetition.
Cyclic time continually comes full circle commemorating events like
a liturgy. This aspect of time was acknowledged and revered by the
ancients. New Year, in early times, coincided with the expulsion of
demons and purification of the universe. It was a repetition of the
original creation, an abolition of history as linear. New birth in-
cluded death and resurrection, an eternal return. Death is necessary
for life to happen and for the cycle to continue. The moon is a symbol of this cycle since it appears, waxes, wanes, disappears, and reap-
pears.

Synchronicity brings cyclic time into historical time. As we saw
earlier, events to the ancients were not irreversible and thus not historical in our sense. In cyclic time everything begins over again at
every moment. The year becomes a holy-day cycle of our own ever-
recurring journey. "No event is irreversible and no transformation is
final. . . . The desire to refuse history testifies to man's thirst for the
real and his terror of losing himself by being overwhelmed by the
meaninglessness of profane existence," says Mircea Eliade in *The
Myth of the Eternal Return*.

In ancient paleo-Oriental religions, revelation happened in
mythic time, before the beginning of the world, and then was repeated in an archetypal way. In monotheism, revelation happens at
a specific time and place, for example, Moses on Sinai. Events of

revelation become precious since they are no longer repeatable but happening once and for all in a historic moment. In that perspective, time is full of hope because it grants us a continuing opportunity for redemption.

Joseph Campbell proposes that "true mysticism releases you from time and then returns you to it." This is the conception of time as *kairos,* which in Homeric Greek means "a penetrable opening." A *kairos* is a time of immediate opportunity, especially an opportunity for spiritual transformation. Synchronicity makes any moment a *kairos* since it connects us to destiny.

Kairos in ancient Greece was personified as the god of lucky coincidence (serendipity). Aion was the god of time, originally a vital fluid in all beings. *Aion* refers to eternal time, the *nunc stans*: the timeless moment beyond the flux of change. Aion does not abolish time but enlivens it spiritually. Since this time cannot be distinguished from normal time, we are confronted with a combination of opposites, exactly the paradoxical precinct of synchronicity, most appealing to the Self and most scary to the ego.

The Self speaks to us in dreams and synchronicity, showing us that there is no serial time: past first, then present, then future. All time is simultaneous and inseparable in an unboundedly timeless present. This is beyond the conceptual limits of the rational, left-brain mind for which time can only be a succession of past to present to future. Synchronicity is freedom from such succession.

Here is an example that may clarify how it is possible to enter this other sense of time. Yesterday I watched a DVD that you are watching today. In the middle of your watching it, I walk in and I instantly recall the scene you are seeing. I know what will happen to the characters on the screen in this scene and in the rest of the film. I know this without having to take time to think about it. I know all the fates of all the characters and the plot too, in one moment. I do not have to wait to know scene by scene as you do. You know the present of the movie and the past (beginning part) of it. You do not know the future (how it will end). You are watching in serial time. This is how the rational ego experiences time. In the example, I am watching in simultaneity, something like the way the inner Self can experience time as timelessness. Synchronicity is a timely moment that takes us beyond the limits of time.

Past and future are opposites in the conscious rational mind and cannot be united. In the Self, opposites are joined and the limitations of serial, time-bound knowing are suspended. Mystics lived in this same time-liberated way. These two elements are what make us refer to this synchronous way of knowing as spiritual.

Our task, as always, is twofold, psychological and spiritual, to fulfill the demands of clock time and to honor the unbound rhythms of the Self. We work out our destiny in hours and days and are escorted to it at special moments under a sky of timelessness. We are consciously aware of clock time here and now and not of simultaneity/eternity. Occasionally it is noticed, and that is synchronicity.

In the fifteenth century, a clock was seen as a model of the divine plan of creation and redemption. The clock was actually revered as a religious phenomenon until the eighteenth century. Thereafter it was considered only a machine. A clock is a mandala in the spiritual perspective. Time is yang and space is yin. Together, they manifest the Tao, the harmonious law governing the universe, the meaning behind appearances. Time is a means of actualizing the Tao since we work in time and sometimes see eternity manifesting in time/space events. In linear time we are spinning out something new from what is not here yet. In moments of synchronicity we are unfolding what was always here. This is the same time-transcendent consciousness by which we discover and experience the spiritual world.

The Egyptian god Aker, whose name means "this moment," was represented by two lions sitting back to back. The sun was shown over the point of their connection. The lions' names were "Yesterday" and "Tomorrow." They are the synchronicity of simultaneous time connected in the present while including the past and future. They were the doorkeepers of the underworld, the guardians of the threshold into spiritual consciousness. In mythology, the conjunction of opposites is the gate to the underworld. It was believed that the death and rebirth of the sun occurred at midnight, that the transforming moment happened in the dark—where the dough also rises. In medieval alchemy the new moon was the time of the conjunction of opposites and of new life. All this is synchronicity, the moment/threshold that joins time and the timely, time and timelessness. The fact that we experience synchronicity is a proof, or rather gift, that we were meant for spirituality.

Since enlightenment can happen at any moment, time is so much more than a series of hours. It is the gate through which our mortality finds a way to meet up with eternity. We cannot hold back the hands of time, but we can be held by them as we stand at the crossroads of every coincidence and then take the path with heart. It all happens in time. "In time" is meant in three senses: in the course of our lifetime, at just the right moment, and in time with the beat of the music of the spheres, those of the earth and sky. Shakespeare says, "Such harmony is in immortal souls."

Finally, in addition to time, number also partakes of synchronicity. Jung wrote, "Number is the most primitive element of order in the human mind." Number is the archetype of order made conscious. Mathematical order manifests the dynamics of the psyche. Number is a symbol of the order of the universe and the oneness of psyche and matter. "Our psyche may have a numerical structure of order that is validated by matter and psyche, both lattices of a numerical field," suggested Marie-Louise Von Franz. An example of this is in the fact that the Fibonacci number series corresponds to the laws of plant growth. For the Chinese, number is the bridge between the timeless and the timely. A synchronous principle of orderly number thus underlies psyche and matter. RNA and DNA (the bases of heredity) use a mathematical code that corresponds to the I Ching hexagrams!

> Attired with stars, I shall forever sit,
> Triumphing over death and chance, and thee, O Time!
> —JOHN MILTON

THE KNACK OF KNOWING OUR TIMING

"To transform itself in us, the future enters into us long before it happens," Rilke wrote. Many psychic events do not occur instantaneously but undergo an incubation period in the unconscious. Something has not yet happened but is in the works. Synchronicity cuts across time-bound limits. It transcends the polarities of being now and becoming soon. This is because in the inner world there is no separation between past and future, time or timelessness, what is happening, what is about to happen, and what will happen. We are always and already perfect in an eternal now and in an only here. Only the present exists, which contains it all. In synchronicity, we meet our future—or our past—in our present. The fact that past events become fully realized in the present means, in effect, that there is no past, only one long now.

Nonetheless, things that matter take time. Impatience is a refusal to honor the built-in timing of events and human decisions or actions. Resistance, in this context, is being unwilling to go with the tide or unreadiness for it. Timing is respect for the necessary incubation period that most transitions and changes require. The ego is not in control of how much time such processes may take. "The revelation knows its own time and will only appear when it cannot possibly be mistaken for anything else," says mystic Bernadette Roberts. Every feeling has its own timing. Grief is the best example. Our attempts as haste or delay are useless as grief unravels and returns in an ever-surprising and often distressing variety of feelings and forms.

No matter how suddenly something may come to pass, it brewed for a long time in silence before it frothed. Timing is a way of referring to the natural incubation period that all births require. To respect timing is to allow that period, that pause in our souls, as new things come to bloom in us. Becoming more loving, wise, and healing is a rebirth of Self from the ashes of the ego. It is a gentle thing and it takes gentleness to allow it. We are not forced by fear or desire into delay or haste. We respect the timing of the self and yet keep gondoliering with optimism and alacrity.

The psyche is a wise system that knows just when to open to the world and when to close off from it. It knows how and when to be born or reborn and when to die. It is calibrated to external events and so synchronicities convene to support it in the direction of opening or of closing. Our healthy ego stabilizes itself through interactions, crisis, conflicts, and any ongoing traffic in the world. These are the vehicles by which we align ourselves to the opening direction. Introspection and meditation are the vehicles for the inward direction. The first keeps the ego permeable and the second keeps it safely intact. What we call depression may be a gross—but perhaps the only—way of closing when other, healthier styles do not seem possible for us. In any case, depression is a constant in the normal ebb and flow of life, nothing to be ashamed of.

Respecting timing means that we adjust to openings and closings. A fully human journey requires a visit to both those sides of the river of timeliness.

There is a time to:	*There is a time to:*
Take hold or hold on	Let go
Fight	Retreat
Take on more cargo	Jettison cargo
Hold a hand	Let go of a hand
Poke	Prompt
Jump to it	Sit with it
Act on logic	Act on faith
Go for it	Wait for it
Enter or join	Make a graceful exit
Be involved	Be alone
Control	Allow
Pull weeds (yank)	Pick figs (tug)

There is a time to:	*There is a time to:*
Speak up	Remain silent
Plan ahead	Be spontaneous
Knead the dough	Let it rise
Know	Not know
Create anew	Repeat again
Break rules	Follow rules
Transcend boundaries	Honor boundaries
Show male/yang energy	Show female/yin energy
Hit	Bunt
Use time industriously	Allow some idling
Feel whole	Feel fragmented
Reconstitute, resurrect	Fall apart, disintegrate
Make a choice	Take a chance
Achieve by effort	Receive grace
Do	Be

The left is active; the right is receptive. Both sides have a gift dimension. Both are initiatory *and* consolatory. Yin and yang are indelible features of the human psyche. In every archetypal story, we see the hero exploring both shores of the river of experience. Our ego makes us fear or feel ashamed of visits to the right side. We may trust only effort and activity. Is this because we have noticed its noise-making drowns out our panic about the gap, the void that opens when we are not in full control? Is this what makes us more at home with changing things than with accepting things?

> There is a tide in the affairs of men,
> Which, taken at the flood, leads on to fortune;
> Omitted, all the voyage of their life
> Is bound in shallows and in miseries.
> On such a full sea are we now afloat;

And we must take the current when it serves,
Or lose our ventures.

—WILLIAM SHAKESPEARE, *Julius Caesar*

THE EMBRACE OF EFFORT AND GRACE

The Self cannot be gained by the Vedas, nor by understanding, nor by learning. He whom the Self chooses, by him
the Self is gained. Nor is that Self to be gained by one who
is destitute of strength or without earnestness or right
meditation. . . . The wise, having reached him who is present
everywhere, enter him wholly.

—UPANISHADS

There is nothing to be attained, yet I engage in action.

—BHAGAVAD GITA

Our psychological work requires effort: handling fear; practicing as-
sertiveness; dealing with inner child issues; addressing, processing,
and resolving concerns in life and relationships; etc. Our spiritual
practice requires effort: meditation, mindfulness, rituals, prayer,
loving-kindness and compassionate action, etc. As we saw above,
these are the equivalent of kneading dough. But for bread to result,
there has to be a period of rising, in which work ceases and nature
takes over. This is the equivalent of grace, a force that takes over
where will, effort, and intelligence leave off. It is a mysterious en-
dowment not a result of the work, yet it often cannot happen without the work, as our quotation from the Upanishads attests.

Both effort and grace are necessary for personal integration—as
both psychological work and spiritual practice are necessary for
wholeness. Effort is a choice; grace is a free gift, beyond our control
or ability to predict. It cannot be conjured up at our initiative. The
best we can do is simply to place ourselves in an apt position for
grace to occur. Ultimately, however, effort may not yield transfor-

mation and grace may come our way with no effort at all. The muses are personifications of grace. Any writer knows that the muse cannot be seduced by our effort though we work hard anyway. The Greek poet Pindar refers to this mystery when he says, "If happiness is at all possible to us, it will take struggle. Yet a god may grant it to us even now."

Here is a chart that may help show the connection between effort and grace based on what we have seen so far.

Ego: conscious, existential	*Self: unconscious, essential*
Works personally by effort toward the goal of functioning optimally in relationships, in a career, and within oneself	Works spiritually by grace toward a destiny to release riches of love, wisdom, and healing into the world
Leads to higher self-esteem and effectiveness because we change	Leads to enlightenment because we are transformed
Is told in our personal story	Is told in myth and metaphor
Presents challenges to make things happen	Asks only cooperation with what wants to happen
Is a cause that leads to an effect	Is synchronous simultaneity
Is based on steps we take	Is based on shifts that happen

Grace, as we have been seeing, is the advocate archetype, the assisting force that helps the hero when he has nothing going for him but his limited ego. It is often symbolized as the aid of a god or an elixir, a talisman, or some form of magic. Grace is that which cannot be willed by ego; it is a free gift of the universe/God/Higher Power/Amitabha Buddha. We may instruct ourselves in knowledge using our intellect, but wisdom is a gift. We may progress in spiritual practice, but enlightenment is a gift. The attitude for work is to gird our loins; the attitude for grace is letting go. Now we see that letting go of ego is transcendence.

In Alcoholics Anonymous, recovery requires a spiritual program. Willpower will not suffice. A Higher Power refers to a source of power beyond what ego is capable of, that which transcends the limits of intellect and will. Our overly controlling ego will never yield only to effort. It takes grace to surrender it. This is the concept of the twelve steps in Alcoholics Anonymous. "I am powerless" is an admission that ego is insufficient. "The Higher Power that can restore me to sanity" is the grace that picks up where the willpower of ego leaves off. We are already and always fitting vehicles for the light, thanks to the action of grace. Honest self-acceptance is thus an opening to grace.

Every one of us is like Pinocchio in the Disney cartoon. We were not born real; it is something we have to achieve by effort and receive by grace. At first we think becoming real/healthy/whole means being dutiful: "Go to school and follow your conscience"—things we can control. Soon we find it takes more than that. We have to confront our dark side. We have to notice how we lie, how we look for a quick fix, how we still believe our addictions can content us in ice-cream land. Then we find out that we have to go into the belly of the whale, the depths of the unconscious, and be inventive enough to light a fire to help others live. Only then are we reborn from the dark, that is, spit out of the whale's mouth. Then and only then are we ready to become real, but we are still not real yet. We cannot achieve the final part of the transformation on our own. The Blue Fairy has to lean lovingly over the body of a broken boy, a disassembled, dissolved ego ready for rebirth. The Blue Fairy (feminine intervention) represents the grace that makes us whole. Effort (masculine power) was not enough, not even heroic effort. It takes the wand of grace to tap us in its own time for the process to be complete. The reality of liberation is achieved *and* received. We saw all this in the childhood cartoon. Now, in this paragraph, we see *into* it in a new way. This too is synchronicity.

Before the work, before the journey, we are still only makeshift persons, headpieces filled with straw, parts held together with ego's unreliable mucilage. We are all wooden heads until we achieve a crossing of the thresholds of F. A. C. E. and receive the beatific vision of grace. Achievement may only congratulate and inflate the ego; grace reminds the ego of its limitations and then joyously completes it. Spiritual materialism is the illusion that enlightenment will happen by effort. Spiritual sanity and spiritual adulthood see past the omnipotent theatrics of ego and show gratitude for the play of grace.

Pinocchio's story is a myth of our childhood. Joseph Campbell says, "The images of myth are reflections of the spiritual potentialities of every one of us. Through contemplating these, we evoke their powers in our lives." As another childhood example, we have the story of the sword in the stone, Excalibur, which tells us that spiritual power is hidden in the dark and can be released with ease if it is our destiny to release it. The special capacity comes only to the one who fits *this* story: only Arthur can free Excalibur, not knights from other ancestries or Prince Charmings from other tales. Our personal story is an apt birthplace for transformation.

Arthur can only grasp the sword when the time is right. An essential feature of grace is certainly timing, the corollary of synchronicity. The chick cannot break out of her shell until her beak is firm enough to crack it. Only then will her effort in pecking at the shell yield liberation from it. The timing is graceful and synchronous in that the food supply in the egg ends at precisely the time the chick is ready to emerge. This is also a metaphor for the work we achieve and the perfect grace we receive to make our work effective.

Timing also means pacing. Babies pace their birth unless they are rushed through it, in which case they suffer a birth trauma because they cannot track—feel the coherence of—their experience. Our respect for our own timing makes it possible for us to track ourselves and process our life events. This is how we become conscious and gain a sense of personal power.

Grace often enters the hero story at the moment when the time has come for the hero to acknowledge his inadequacy. This is the dismemberment theme; we find ourselves in pieces. A force comes to us that takes us beyond our own limits and enlarges us, that is, makes us whole. A hero story seems to require constant action, but within the struggle phase there is always a period of captivity, a pause that allows other forces to come into play. Robin Hood takes action, but then he is in chains until Maid Marian helps him. Even the dungeon, that is, the void, is part of the path.

We think back on what we consider our wasted, unconscious years. Were they perhaps the rising of the dough, the necessary darkness? Were they the necessary pause, like the one before the finale of fireworks? This is an appropriate metaphor since what is a pause to us watching from afar is a busy time to the pyrotechnician whose operations we do not see but whose results astonish us.

Another threshold of grace is in the hero's sometime inability to perform the task at hand. This is a metaphor of how the psyche is sometimes unconscious of her powers. An example is the miller's daughter unable to turn straw to gold in *Rumplestiltskin* or Psyche's inability to sort the diverse grains that Aphrodite presented to her in Greek mythology. The ego is incapacitated because the Self is unready or asleep. Grace is the awakening of hidden powers. A legitimate part of the heroic struggle is containment. Sometimes the task is to hide or sleep. The ego's work is simply to sit, be taken blindfolded, or be under spell. Examples are Jack in the cupboard of the giant's wife, Snow White in her glass casket, Christ in his tomb, Dorothy asleep among the poppies, and Joseph in Pharaoh's prison. This is not wasted time but the simmering necessary for the consommé to be ready. It is also the dough rising in the dark, like dreaming in which psychological and spiritual work are being done while we remain unconscious.

We fear a visit to the far side of the ego, where control dissolves and action is ineffective. Quiet gaps seem ominous, boring, or lacking the adrenaline rush to which we are accustomed or addicted. We fear having no story, no identity if there is no dramatic excitement. Yet marvels happen best in the pause between plot developments. This pause is serene attentiveness: "Be still and know." At the same time, we hear a summons to activate ourselves: "Be swift my

soul . . . be jubilant my feet!"These recommendations seem contradictory but only to the linear intellect. In the psyche's world they
deftly combine apparently opposing but truly legitimate phases of
our work. The result of such a combination happening in us is the
inner rainbow with its shades of bright and dun to release the full
spectrum of the light.

> The key to our deepest happiness lies in changing our vision
> of where to find it.
> —SHARON SALZBERG, *Lovingkindness*

WHEN THE TIME IS ALL WRONG

> As I sat there brooding on the old, unknown world, I thought
> of Gatsby's wonder when he first picked out the green light
> at the end of Daisy's dock. . . . He did not know then that it
> was already behind him.
> —F. SCOTT FITZGERALD, *The Great Gatsby*

Asynchrony is the opposite of synchronicity. The timing of events or
opportunities is mismatched with safety, creativity, or positive results. Things do not work out because the time has not come. We may
then become aware, through a series of negating coincidences, that
this is the wrong time for ventures. Nothing works; doors keep closing; obstacles arise that are not challenges but blockades. If we fight
on, we find ourselves involved in wars of attrition, forced to obey
laws of diminishing returns.

At the end of *King Lear,* the Duke of Albany offers to share his
authority with Kent and Edgar, both of whom refuse:

> KENT: "I have a journey, sir, shortly to go / My master calls
> me; I must not say no."
> EDGAR: "The weight of this sad time we must obey. . . ."

Both characters read their own times accurately. Reading the handwriting on the wall is often a way of describing a respect for asynchrony. Accepting the given of change and endings makes us aware that our time is almost up and we are ready for new options elsewhere. We have to tune our ear to be able to distinguish reveille from taps. We can yank the figs from the tree in early summer and find only an insipid taste. The message in the lack of sweetness is "not now but later." In late summer and early fall, the figs will yield with ease to the slightest tug, that is, they will be synchronously sweet.

Asynchrony is also a challenge to the "little engine that could" or the "any man can be president" ego-inflating (or ultimately ego-deflating) mentality that we may have inherited from public school. The danger is in the absolutizing of those messages in such a way that trying hard becomes the only acceptable plan. It is sometimes true that effort is expedient. However, it is also sometimes true that letting go for now or for good is necessary. We were not meant to win all the time; we learn from losing too, so we get that chance. For those in tune with the universe, messages will come to us in synchronicity, in dreams, and in inner images that reveal which is the appropriate path. It will not be based on maxims but on the maximum series of messages that point to a particular path.

Asynchrony appears in relationships in a variety of ways. It is in the mismatching and incompatibility of some partners. It shows itself in frustrating games of intimacy and distance between partners: I draw near when you pull back, and vice versa. We may keep doing what does not work no matter how we try. We may stay in a relationship that cannot work no matter what we do. Asynchrony can appear in a relationship when one partner fears abandonment so much that he continually clings while the other partner feels engulfed and goes away even more.

Sometimes, synchronicity and asynchrony combine in differing directions. At the end of *Romeo and Juliet* we discover that what is asynchrony for the young couple is synchronicity for their families. A harsh end for Romeo and Juliet leads to a reconciliation for the rest of the family. Our own lives show interstices like that, especially in relationships. We endure pain with no possibility of change, and when we finally believe we have a right to happiness and we move on, the pain becomes a path to personal growth.

Paying attention is the first requisite for finding asynchrony. The second is letting go of the inflated ego belief that "it has to be my way," or the belief that "it has to be one way." I cannot force a butterfly to emerge before its time. I cannot successfully pull the budded petals of the rose away to make it look as if it were in bloom.

PRACTICING IN TIME

1. Look at the time it took for you to work through the important issues in your life, to find the solutions to the important questions, even to know the questions. Look at the time it took to meet the people who could teach you just what you needed to learn, especially in relationships. How are you respecting or dishonoring your timing now? Do you allow time to take its course and remain patient while at the same time arising to action in a timely way? Find an example and practice this blending of movement and pause. Classical ballet uses precisely that same alternating combination.

2. Our timing is respected by simmering. Here is the test of time in the making of important choices: having to want something for thirty days straight before you trust that you really want it. How would your life be different if you had slept on all your important decisions in that way? Can you commit yourself to such a plan today? Others have timing that may be quite different from yours and may frustrate you. You especially want those you love to move forward and be successful. You sometimes try to force them to move more rapidly than they choose to. Respect of others is shown in respecting their readiness or unreadiness. When someone seems ready and is choosing not to move ahead, it is not appropriate to force or push her, but to grieve and allow.

Gentle encouragement, giving information once, and then a "hands off" policy may work best. Can you apply this to any relationships in your life now?

3. In exploring asynchrony in your life now, do you notice that nothing works or falls into place, one dead end after another? Putting in all the effort you can is a good rule. But when do you draw the line and say, "That's it. It's time to let go and move on"? There is no infallible way to know if you would do better to keep at it or to give up and move on. These criteria of asynchrony may be helpful.

Let it go if your efforts:
Are depleting you and destroying your self-esteem
Becoming dangerous or intrusive to others
Feel forced—kicking against the goad
Yield less and less
Explode in your face over and over
Prevent you from trying a whole new option that awaits
    you elsewhere
Seem anachronistic—no longer in character for you at
    this age or at this level of consciousness
Are based on childhood messages of how you are supposed
    to succeed or be the strong—or weak—one no matter
    what
Contradict the clear message of someone who is saying No
    to you in every way he can as you keep trying for a Yes
Are based on wishful thinking rather than what the record
    shows

Apply the above criteria to something you are trying hard to accomplish: What are you trying to get your children, partner, friends, parents, or work associates to be or become? What are you trying to make yourself into? What are you pushing at achieving with no result? Is this stubbornness or intelligent effort? Ask for feedback from someone you trust.

Asynchrony is often unnoticed. Yet, synchronous graceful exits have dignity. Here are some hints that help us know when it is time to go:

> I give much more than I receive.
> I do more and more and see the success of less and less.
> I feel that I am giving up something rather than giving and receiving something.
> My health is suffering because of the stress of staying.
> Even what I once liked doing—and can do well—is now flat, stale, and uncomfortable.
> I am no longer effective.
> My bliss and enthusiasm are gone.
> I no longer come up with creative ideas or even see alternatives.
> I have been doing too much for too long for too little thanks.
> I work on changing things but nothing gets better.
> Things keep going wrong and never quite right themselves, no matter how much effort I expend.
> I keep finding myself left with my finger in the dike.
> The same ineffective pattern keeps repeating itself.
> Money or prestige has become my central or sole motivation for staying.
> I do not move on because I am afraid to risk a change.
> I see no alternatives to what I have.
> I doubt ever finding anything better than this.
> I have no assisting forces encouraging me to stay.

Does this apply to me in my job, relationship, commitments, etc.? If it does, what is the program for change that I may know exactly how to implement but am not implementing? Take one baby step in that direction and another tomorrow or next week. If you find it extremely difficult to mobilize on your own, consider asking for help from someone you trust or in therapy. Not all the work can be done alone, or else why were we born into a world?

5

Fate or Destiny?

OUR DESTINY FULFILLED

> *We are dragged along by fate to the destiny*
> *we refuse to walk toward upright.*
> —CARL JUNG

Fate often allows a future to take shape with no regard for our expectation, plan, or readiness. Fate's skillful editing of our life choices is like the careful grooming of lads on their first day of school: combed, polished, scrubbed, newly dressed, and glowing too. This is how we become ready for our life lessons.

The ancient Greeks used a personification for fate: the three spinning sisters who decided on the length of each person's thread of life, love, and power. Lachesis controlled the length of the thread; Clotho spun the thread; and Atrophos cut the thread when the time for ending had come. This is a metaphor for the presence of a transcendent force or power that disposes what the ego proposes. Each human project, lifetime, relationship, power bond, consolation, grief, etc., has its own life span. There is a sense of something "greater than" myself that is at work beyond my control. This plan is my *fate* when I am at its mercy, that is, caught off guard, fighting tooth and nail, shaking my fist at heaven. It is my *destiny* when I join in with it with choice, consciousness, and cooperation—although there is no harm in trying to massage and cajole the fates for some extra time too! Synchronicity is what shows me where the thread is leading, how long it is, and who or what in my life is spinning it at the moment.

The culmination of synchronicity is its aptitude for revealing our destiny, which can mean simply our life story or can have the grander scope we are shooting for in this book. Then destiny can be the evolutionary design of the whole universe as it fulfills itself in the daily display of each of our unique human lives. "Life is a struggle to succeed in being in fact what we are in design. . . . Our will is free to realize or not to realize the vital design we are but which we cannot change or abbreviate," wrote the philosopher José Ortega y Gasset.

What we refuse to bring into consciousness comes back to us as fate. It hits us from without when we refuse to heed its summons from within. This is why it makes spiritual sense for us to forge a lasting agreement with the universe, which can only be an unconditional Yes to what is. Attention to synchronicity helps us consciously join the unfolding of what is. Ortega y Gasset's word "design" reminds us of the element of artistry in the unfolding.

As we saw above, there is a lifelong synchronicity in the link between our innate talents or gifts and our life work. Our talents bring us bliss when we follow them up with practice. When bliss and talent come together, we know what our vocation is and we find work that pays our salary. In addition, in our career we meet other people with inclinations and fascinations like our own and from among them come lifelong colleagues, friends, or partners. It all works together in a synchronous way so that who we always were makes who we are and will be one joyous and successful continuity. The synchronicity is complete when we feel grateful for the grace by which it all worked out and we feel a rise in spiritual consciousness.

We gain a sense of fulfillment especially when we notice that our work is making a contribution to our family and to humanity in some way. This is how our inborn interests lead us to our destiny. "My work is that of a collective being and it bears Goethe's name," Goethe wrote. Our work on ourselves makes us healthy enough to transcend our immediate gratifications long enough to make our contribution to the world. This is why compassion is always an essential element of spirituality. "Individuation does not shut out the world but gathers it to oneself," says Jung.

There is synchronicity in the fact that this Class of 2007—every person on earth today—comprises members who, taken together, have everything the world needs for it to evolve fully now. Some of our classmates are models and heroes and some are rogues and rascals. Some are getting *A*s in their work and some are failing. Some love their alma mater and others are attempting to destroy her. As a member of this class, I have a unique contribution that no one else can make but me. I am an indispensable participant in the vast unfolding and protecting of my world. Among those alive this year, there is a precise and ample combination of ingredients and strengths for the nourishment of today's world. It will stand up to those on the dark side. How can I doubt that I have a part to play in this arc of wholeness that moves in such perfect timing toward the eternal commencement? The other people in my life and on the planet now have come to receive my gifts. They are also assisting forces in my self-discovery. Our personal fulfillment requires a wider resource than just ourselves or our family. This alignment of personal and universal purposes is a beautiful example of how synchronicity and destiny go hand in hand. The mountainous desires in our hearts are the desire of the everlasting hills of earth.

Thus it is a synchronous fact that here and now the world always has just the human resources that it needs to further its evolution as is fitting for this epoch. Nature participates in the same synchronicity by its drifts of growth and change in each era, both in seasons and in species. Nature mounts an ice age and a temperate age in accord with the overall requirements of evolution. I am here at the right time—and just in time—for me to make my contribution, and nature is supporting me by presenting just the conditions that promote this enterprise. And so are all the people in my life, both now and in the past.

Jonah is the biblical archetype of refusing one's destiny. Since he was needed as a prophet, his refusal of the call to become one was disregarded by Yahweh. He was swallowed by a whale and thereby forced to swallow his pride. Jung wisely wrote, "We find our destiny on the path we take to avoid it."

There are also times in the course of life when our refusals are allowed to stand and then "a great prince in prison lies," as the poet John Donne says. The greatest of human tragedies is to be distracted from our destiny and lose our power to activate our potential because of years of stuckness, laziness, addictions, or relationships that are abusive, unworkable, or depleting and imprisoning. A great potential in us can thereby fade away, and no one does anything to halt the dissolution. The world will stand by as we throw away our fortune. We will stand by as we throw ourselves away. There is no guarantee that a whale will intervene for us, as it did for Jonah, or a tornado, as it did for Dorothy. The challenge is to find our destiny in exactly what we are refusing to engage in. This is no easy task. It is hard to stop and look while we are running the other way. *Is my real destiny scribbled on parchment, twirled in a bottle and hurled into the sea, to be stumbled upon only long after I am gone?*

Some of our difficulty in finding out who we are and what we are called to be stems from toxic injunctions and imperatives that we introjected. We heard or imbibed perspectives from our parents and others that interrupted our self-emergence. These may have taken the form of verbal messages that negated our power, beliefs that diminished or inhibited us, such as images of what a man/woman *should* be. These three forms of childhood detritus may now litter our psyche so that we cannot walk freely toward our personal destiny. They are generalized myths that do not fit our present reality. They are to be examined and scuttled if they do not serve us, if they disable us, or if they disempower us. Only those messages, beliefs, and images that animate our potential and release it are to be cherished and maintained. Obedience to self-defeating messages, beliefs, and images denies us the chance to be who we are. In such obedience we cannot love ourselves, part of the achievement of which is living out our own destiny. "Whom do I obey?"

A belief system that has despair as its bottom line may be organizing our life experiences and choices. "I am fated to lose," "Nothing I do will ever work out," "I'll never be good enough." These self-negations do not arise from our true self but are an alien cargo that may have been smuggled into our psyches in early life. Before we could discriminate, our parents' worst fears and beliefs may have become such cargo in our minds. To maintain the crucially needed tie with our parents, we may have had to join them in their despair about us/themselves. This happened at the dear price of our own self-authenticated experience of the world. Now optimistic glimmers, encouraging signs, hopeful prospects, and even kind words or compliments fall flat. They land in the quicksand of automatic disbelief and disavowal.

Despair is the illusion that there is an inexorable fate that awaits our condition and our enterprises. Synchronicity tells us there is no such thing as an inexorable fate. Choices continue to arise and paths continue to appear even until the eleventh hour of a lifetime. Even if the path is to grieve an ending, the next step is to go on. Even if it is our ending, are we not still able to salute the sunset with dignity, equanimity, and deeply contented serenity?

In the film *Mr. Holland's Opus*, the main character was a competent instructor of music who helped many young people achieve their potential. Mr. Holland was a born teacher, but he sometimes felt despair because he really wanted to direct a symphony orchestra. Some people may find great success and seem to hit the target of their destiny in a career and all the while they wish it were otherwise. There are no guarantees in the enigmatic world of the Self. We find ourselves not in charge of how it will be for us or in charge of how it has been. We realize that our wishes or even our choices or successes may give us no information about our real destiny. It is a mystery of synchronicity that life/destiny works just right for some and not for others. Synchronicity has a power beyond the ego's will, another way of saying that it is a grace with a will of its own.

The question arises: How am I responsible if things happen to me beyond my control or my will? There is a seemingly contradictory answer to this in the *Iliad*: Agamemnon incites the wrath of Achilles by taking his slave woman from him. Agamemnon later says to Achilles, "Since destiny did this to me, I will give compensation." "What happened was incited by Zeus," adds Achilles. But notice that even though both of them make fate/god responsible for what happened, the liability for amends is nonetheless Agamemnon's. We may not produce the "what is," but we are accountable for how we handle it.

There is no conflict in an enlightened person between what happens and human choice, since there is always a coincidence, an aligning of her personal will and that of the universe. This is articulated in an unconditional Yes to what is. By that Yes, I am the embodiment of nature's laws and harmonies. Shakespeare states this so profoundly in the speech we keep returning to from *The Merchant of Venice*: "Soft stillness and the night become the touches of sweet harmony. . . . Such harmony is in immortal souls."

How to Know What We Want

1. Here are some suggestions that may be helpful in discovering and embracing your own reality and thereby moving toward the fulfillment of your destiny. Following these may help you know who you really are and then know how to act on that knowledge in healthy ways.

   Tell those close to you what you feel within yourself and in reaction to them, no matter how embarrassing it may be.

   If necessary, allow yourself to retreat from a distressing issue long enough to regroup your strengths. Then come back and face the music with a sense of personal power.

Pause to hold every feeling, cradling it, and allowing it to have its full career in you. Distractions and avoidances only conceal you from yourself. We learned early in life to overlook our authentic feelings so as not to "hurt the feelings" of others. This stop-and-hold method reverses that misguided self-sacrifice.

Embrace this triple-A program for handling fear: **a**dmit your fear, **a**llow yourself to feel it, and then **a**ct as if it were not able to stop or drive you.

Some fears are obstacles to what you really want. Other fears are signals that you are attempting something that you do not want. For example, you may fear commitment to a partner. If that fear is a hurdle to jump in your own evolution, apply the program above to *fulfill* your authentic needs and wishes. If that fear is a warning to you that you are not cut out for a committed relationship but only for lighter ones, then take the fear as *information* about your authentic needs and wishes. How can you tell the difference? Simply let the record speak. How have you mostly operated in your relationships? What has mostly worked? Fear thrives on isolation, trappedness, and powerlessness. Admitting fear reduces ego and ends isolation since the more deeply personal a feeling is, the more definitely will you trust that it is widely felt by fellow pilgrims.

2. There is a connection between self-knowledge and self-esteem. Consider these three pegs of self-esteem and how they fit for you.

First: Act in the most loving way you can toward everyone.

Second: Build a sense of accomplishment based on your doing all you can with your talents and potential. This will usually require discipline and patience as you work on gaining the credentials to do the work that can fulfill you.

Third: Grant yourself the freedom to act and live in accord with your deepest wishes and needs. This is the secret of finding out who you really are, free of injunctions and inhibitions from childhood. Here are some ways of knowing what your wishes and needs really are:

- Free yourself from inhibition and clinging and see what results.
- Tell the truth about yourself. Self-disclosure leads to self-knowing.
- Ask often for what you already know you want and gradually you will ask yourself—and others—for the deeper things.
- Set boundaries in your relationships and you will know a great deal about yourself and your real needs. In a truly healthy relationship, you do not have to submerge, deny, or kill off any of your deepest needs and wishes.
- Ask before each venture, Does this make me happy and give me a sense of fulfillment? Notice how many *yeses* follow or how many *nos*.
- What are you doing in life that flows from blissful choice, and what is based on a sense of obligation or habit? Resolution: "I will make no choices or promises that repudiate or discount my true needs and desires."
- Look at the record. The history of what you have actually done in the course of your life tells you more about yourself than the fantasy of what you wish you had done or what you say you want.
- If you acted with the highest level of consciousness, health, and spirituality, how would your life be different? The difference probably reveals what you truly want and need.
- What you strongly admire in others may be what you want—and can accomplish too.
- What you want for your children and best friends may tell you what you want.

- Consider the ingredients of your present life, for example, relationship, housing, job, friends, diet, etc. Plot yourself on the following spectrum to see just how much your choices reflect your real wishes. Move from dislike to indifference, interest, enthusiasm, excitement.
- Make an inventory of your fears. On the other side of the coin of fear is an excitement/risk that is un-lived. There lie our disenfranchised feelings, wishes, and needs.
- Where do your dreams and synchronicity lead you?

Respond to each of the entries in the above list, noticing which feelings, wants, and needs come through most frequently.

3. Look at the major life choices you have made: Were they based on the messages, beliefs, and images from others or from yourself? Have you looked at them consciously and then deliberately chosen them? Are you carrying someone else's myth, an alien presence inside? The work is to clear yourself of false and self-defeating myths. Do this by looking at what has worked for you, that is, what has led to bliss and success. What has failed? Which of these has been scuttled and which has been maintained?

Destiny comes from the Latin word meaning "to determine." It is used in the following senses: to set the time and place for a battle, to resolve to do something, to set the time for an execution, to ordain someone to an office, to aim a weapon, to betroth as a wife, to fix one's sights on something worth buying, to act intentionally. The definitions are all deliberate and conscious, denoting destiny not as something forced upon us but as something consciously sought. Look over your life story and notice three ways destiny seemed to happen to you and three ways in which you had a hand in what happened to you. Look more carefully later and find a similarity in all six.

At this point, you may notice synchronicities happening more frequently in your daily life. Reading this book and being on the lookout for them can attract them to you.

A Fateful Tale

This is a story, probably apocryphal, full of synchronicities about a medieval Catholic saint. It is an example of how fate can lead to destiny when the ego becomes humble:

Julian, a haughty young nobleman, was out hunting one day deep in the forest when he was suddenly confronted by a mysterious white stag. Julian was startled and bewildered when the stag began to speak: "You will not slay me but someday you will slay your parents!" Profoundly troubled, and not ever wanting such a fate to befall him, Julian rode off secretly that very night far from his parents' home. After a long and arduous journey, he found himself in another kingdom. His skill with weapons soon distinguished him to all, and after a while he was invited to join the king's personal guard.

The king could not help but recognize Julian's prowess in battle, his proud integrity, his noble bearing, and even the strange poignant sadness that occasionally became visible in his face and made him seem more mature than his young years accounted for. The king soon knighted Julian and thereafter gave him a castle and even his daughter's hand in marriage. Princess Catherine was beautiful and known for her piety and kindness to the poor. On their wedding night, Catherine inquired of her husband about his origins. Julian honestly confided to her about the prophecy and his self-imposed exile. She felt compassion for his shackles of superstition and fear and hoped that he would learn to trust God's providence.

Meanwhile, over these past two years, Julian's parents, grief-stricken and baffled by his departure, had gone searching for him far and wide. One night, while Julian was out hunting with his men, his parents, wearied by the day's travels, found themselves at the gate of his castle, unaware that it was the residence of their son. Princess

Catherine greeted the strangers and invited them in. She was always kind to wayfarers and pilgrims who came to her door. As they sat together drinking ale by the fire, the old folks told the princess of their long search. As Catherine listened, she realized that these were indeed her husband's parents! What a wonderful surprise it would be for them to be greeted by Julian on the morrow! Telling them nothing yet, she gave them her own bridal bed and went to the chapel to offer thanks for such a synchronicity.

That same night, while camping in the woods, Julian overheard two of his men whispering about his wife. Not recognizing the falsity of their statement that she was unfaithful and kept a lover, he saddled his horse and rode at breakneck speed to the castle, his insulted and inflated ego all afire with revenge. Arriving before dawn—his wife by then having dozed off in the chapel—Julian ran breathlessly to the bedroom and indeed saw the outlines of two figures in an embrace under the silken quilt. He dispatched them both with sudden and spiteful blows of his sword as he shrieked with rage and indignation. This brought Catherine from the chapel with a torch, revealing to them both the shameful bloody fulfillment of the stag's somber prophecy.

Julian and Catherine grieved together, and as a penance, they turned their castle into a hospital for the poor. The lame, diseased, and dispossessed came from all over the kingdom to partake of their loving hospitality. Many found healing at the hands of their humble and ingenuous host who, today, is Saint Julian, the patron of hotel keepers.

No Room for Chance

> There is no room for chance in the meaningful world of the psyche.
>
> —Carl Jung

Chance is the unpredictable, unexpected, uncontrollable, and unknown element in events that surprises us happily or shocks us unhappily. It has no explanatory cause. It is a random event in that there is no recognizable pattern or plan behind it. Yet the psychoanalyst Heinz Kohut was perhaps referring to something that transcends chance when he spoke of "the healing power of the random array." Synchronicity takes chance occurrences and relates them to our destiny by the meaningfulness that emerges from or because of them. This is how synchronicity goes for higher stakes than mere chance or only luck.

Chance or luck is mere coincidence, that is, synchronization. Synchronicity is meaningful, life-affecting, destiny-promoting, spiritually encouraging coincidence. Chance and synchronicity will look the same in their display of an event but they are worlds apart. What makes chance into synchronicity is the consciousness in us of the vaster design that is unfolding. Chance happens to us; synchronicity happens in us. Chance and luck are the escorts of synchronicity when we greet them with attention. This is another way of seeing the necessary nexus between synchronicity and consciousness.

Chance or luck are often the words of those who do not honor or believe in spiritual consciousness. Some people deny the reality of the spiritual or the transcendent altogether, ascribing all events in life to chance or luck. Yet chance and luck are actually transcendent too since they occur beyond the control of effort or ego. Chance might then be a minimalist word for synchronicity, as luck is a minimalist word for grace. There is a way out of our mortal world, but thankfully, there is no way out of the spiritual world.

Within this context is the spiritually founded belief that in synchronicity, more is going on than meets the eye; behind the appearance of randomness is an order, and this order wants to manifest. This belief does not necessarily entail theism. One can lay aside the traditional concept of a personal God and still believe in an implicate order in the universe that works itself out in each of us in unique ways. This orderly calibration of the universe has as its goal the harmony of mankind and nature, person and person, matter and spirit. *Something, we know not what, is acting, we know not how, in every heart—*

but we do know why: to release into the existential world the essential reality of love, wisdom, and healing. The Tao expresses it this way: "There is something formless yet complete that existed before heaven and earth. How still! How empty! Dependent upon nothing, unchanging, all pervading, unfailing. . . . I call it meaning." That meaning is synchronicity.

Actually, chance and order work together. A striking example of this is in the proportion of men and women in the world. There is no major disparity in the numbers of each—though there are more women. The gender of a fetus is based on chance, and yet some other force is at work that keeps the population reasonably equalized. The law of probabilities is at work in this, numbers reflecting and even fostering the order in the universe by its correlation with chance.

Chance may simply be a playful way the universe has of collaborating with us in the working out of our destiny. Thus synchronicity integrates the irrational into an organized procession of evolution. The challenge is always the same: to believe in the meaningful design in spite of the random display. The record shows us humans to be crassly ignorant and destructive but also touchingly responsive and restorative. Perhaps Gandhi expressed this tension between our existential display and our essential design most accurately: "I see that mankind still survives after all its attempts to destroy itself and so I surmise that it is the law of love that rules mankind."

> Heaven from all creatures hides the Book of Fate,
> All but the page prescribed, their present state . . .
> O blindness to the future, kindly given,
> That each may fill the circle marked by heaven:
> Who sees with equal eye, as God of all,
> A hero perish and a sparrow fall,
> Atoms or systems into ruin hurled,
> And now a bubble burst and now a world.
> —ALEXANDER POPE, *Essay on Man*

Ways of Foretelling

Is synchronicity a form of superstition? Superstition is an irrational belief in a cause/effect connection when there is none in reality, for example, a belief that a black cat crossing one's path produces bad luck. Synchronicity is based on a reason-transcending meaning, not an irrational belief. Superstition is maintained by ignorance of the laws of nature or by false faith in magic or random chance. Synchronicity is supported by a long-standing wisdom about the correlation between a coincidence and something spiritual that is underway. Examples of this appear in divination devices such as the *I Ching* or Tarot cards. One ineluctably chooses the hexagram or card that coincides with one's circumstance. This meaningful connectedness is based on the belief that the psyche will direct us to the exact information that we need when we need it.

The *I Ching* is the ancient Chinese "Book of Changes." It is a resource text that one turns to with questions about one's life choices, and it works entirely by synchronicity. The inquirer casts yarrow stalks or throws coins to determine the section of the book that speaks precisely and accurately to his life situation. The philosophy of the *I Ching* states that all human affairs are governed by a single law, that of change. This inclination toward change has a geometry. It displays itself in sixty-four processes in the form of graphic hexagrams. When our personal choices align with these processes, harmony results between us and the universe. This means that we are living out our destiny.

In this Chinese approach to reality, the locus of mutability is the center of the universe. This center is perfectly still, yet from it ripples out the many and constant changes we see. It is the same design as that of the mandala, a oneness that allows, generates, and transcends duality. The *I Ching* is based on the belief that coincidence is instructive and that our hand throwing the coins is the psyche that will direct us to the exact information we need. The book/process is a resource of the soul since it addresses the point at which conscious and unconscious meet, a definition of soul.

Jung considered the *I Ching* the best expression of the synchronicity principle: "The Chinese mind, as I see it at work in the *I Ching*, seems to be exclusively preoccupied with the chance aspect of events. What we call coincidence seems to be the chief concern of this peculiar mind, and what we worship as causality passes almost unnoticed. . . . While the Western mind carefully sifts, weighs, selects, classifies, isolates, the Chinese picture of the moment encompasses everything down to the minutest nonsensical detail, because all of the ingredients make up the observed moment."

The Tarot deck is a pack of seventy-eight cards: a Major Arcana of twenty-two trump cards, including a joker/fool, that is, a trickster, and a Minor Arcana of fifty-six cards in four suits—coins or pentacles, scepters or wands, chalices, and swords.

The cards of the Major Arcana correspond to the letters of the Hebrew alphabet and depict archetypal and alchemical figures, virtues, and metaphors that were originally meant to be contemplated and studied as indicators of wholeness. In the seventeenth century, they became pointers to where human fortunes lie. The figures appear in this order in the deck: magician, archpriestess, empress, emperor, archpriest, lover, chariot, justice, hermit, wheel of fortune, strength, the hanged man, death, temperance, devil, tower struck by lightning, stars, moon, sun, judgment, world, and finally or first, the fool. The cards present an image of the path to destiny through initiation.

The suits of the Minor Arcana also represent archetypal forces. The coin stands for the material forces in the world, the scepter for the power of authority, the chalice for sacrifice, and the sword for the dispensing of justice. In each suit there is a king, queen, knight, and knave (jack), representing the categories of earthly power. Scepters stand for government; the military is represented by swords; the priesthood is indicated by a chalice; and coins are for intellectual and aesthetic pursuits.

Cards zero through eleven of the Major Arcana lead us on the solar way: active, conscious, a masculine style. Cards twelve through twenty-one show the lunar way: passive, unconscious, the feminine mystique. Each image combines the inner and outer world in the context of human experiences. The intention of the deck is to present a full panoply of the archetypal possibilities in every human being and show him/her the next or future turn of the road to the activation of those potentials. The Tarot is thus an album of pictures of us, and each of us is the full deck.

Astrology is another rich source of synchronicity in its study of the direct and meaningful coincidence between the layout of the stars and the blueprint of our lives. In a letter to Freud in 1911, Jung wrote, "I dare say that we shall one day discover in astrology a good deal of knowledge that has been intuitively projected into the heavens."

World movements and events correlate synchronously with astrological conditions. Planets and constellations mirror and predict world movements like the Renaissance or World Wars. There is also personal synchronicity in astrology since our psyche is mirrored in the night sky of our birth and of our unfolding life. The unconscious indeed contains planets (gods) as archetypes. All the planets together make up the unconscious, which is a pageant of archetypal figures familiar from all the stories we have read and resonated with: Mars is the hero, Jupiter the king, Venus the female anima-soul, Uranus the male animus-spirit, Saturn the father and conservator, Mercury the trickster, Moon the persona, and Sun individuation. Body, heart, and mind correspond to pairings of gods. The body corresponds to a pairing of Mercury and Venus; the emotions correspond to a pairing of Mars and Jupiter; and the mind corresponds to a pairing of Saturn and Uranus. "I find my zenith doth depend upon a most auspicious star, whose influence / If now I count not, but omit, my fortunes will ever after droop," says Shakespeare in The Tempest.

In medieval times, Saint Albert the Great, inspired by the Persian mystic Ibn Sina, said that the psyche has the power to alter external matter and things when it is in highly charged emotional states and when a favorable astrological pattern coincides with it. For the year to be complete and nature to work, the interaction of all the signs are necessary. Likewise, humanity requires a population with all the astrological signs for the wholeness of the human community. A jury was originally made up of twelve men, each with a different astrological sign to ensure fairness and complete amplitude in judgment.

The zodiac ("circle of animals") contains twelve symbols that indicate the terrestrial situation when the sun is in a particular part of the sky. Aries, the ram, indicates spring; Taurus, the bull, the growth of plants and mating of animals; Gemini, the twins, the proliferation of life within an ecological whole. Cancer, the crab, indicates that the sap of life flows copiously; Leo, the sun's fiery power; Virgo, the harvest and seed for the next year. Libra, the balancing scales, appears at the autumnal equinox, which leads to Scorpio, the sign of death. Sagittarius is the archer of reflection since he looks back as he rides into the winter solstice; Capricorn, with fishtail and goat body, represents a transition from old to new as the sun climbs again; Aquarius, the water-pourer, appears as rains come in winter. Pisces, the fish, indicating living but hidden growth beneath the watered earth, precedes Aries and lilac spring again.

The psyche is indeed like a solar system: instincts, emotions, and thoughts orbit the luminaries of the Self and ego. The sun represents consciousness and moon the unconscious. They are the inner and outer faces of the human psyche. The planets are operational principles of action, heart, and mind. Heaven and earth have definite connections: our blood flow and coagulation correlates with the moon as do the tides. "As above, so below" is the medieval alchemical way of saying this. Uranus represents breaking away from the familiar to embrace the new. It is thus the planet that represents synchronicity. Uranus is the divine intervention that introduces unexpected changes and reversals through unusual people and events that meet us on our path. *Can I meet the unexpected with nothing but space between it and me?*

On the opening page of this book we read Shakespeare's words: "Look how the floor of heaven is thick inlaid with patens of bright gold . . . such harmony is in immortal souls!" The human psyche contains all the stars and planets as metaphors of our full potential. They are not only heavenly bodies but macrocosms of our individual microcosm. We are composed of and highly responsive to their every orbit and vibration. We respond because we are made in their image. The heavens *mirror* us and we are truly children of the stars, terrestrial reflections of celestial constellations. Luke 10:20 states, "Rejoice that your names are written in heaven."

> The call may have been more like gentle pushings in the stream in which you drifted unknowingly to a particular spot on the bank. Looking back, you sense that fate had a hand in it.
>
> —James Hillman

6

Conditions and Crises

THE GIVENS OF HUMAN LIFE

In my book *The Five Things We Cannot Change and the Happiness We Find by Embracing Them* (Shambhala, 2005), I present some givens of life and how to respond to them. In this chapter I look at those and other givens to show how they apply to synchronicity.

The conditions of our human existence can be embraced with acceptance or opposed with rebelliousness. A healthy adult accepts conditions when it is clear that they are irreversible. At the same time, he also may struggle to change a particular condition if it yields to change. Grace provides the wisdom to know the difference. The center column lists the givens of life, the conditions of our human existence. On either side, we see two possible responses.

Adult response	Givens	Childish reaction
I stay with myself and focus on what is and open myself to support if it comes my way	I am alone in facing the great life events, including death. I may have support but no rescuer	I fill the aloneness with externals so as not to feel it fully, or I expect a rescuer
I stay with the normal stages: rise, crest, decline, realign, let go	All is transitory and changing. Nothing satisfies permanently	I fixate: holding on, becoming addicted, clinging, controlling. I keep trying to hold back the hands of time
I allow it all to unfold just as it is	Life is unpredictable	I seek safe harbors and certitudes, trying to build dikes or dams
I accept what cannot be changed; I attend to what can be changed	Suffering is part of life: both physical and emotional life is not always fair	I am entitled to immunity. I am exempt from the law of averages. I deserve special treatment
I accept that things are not always fair while working for justice	Sometimes we will be faced with more than we can handle	I am comforted by the belief that punishment of evil and reward of good will happen now or later
I accept that some things are too big for me to handle		I will never have more to face than I can handle

These are not just the conditions of existing; they are the conditions of evolving. They are the prerequisites for a human life to unfold with character, purpose, and meaning. They make us the fascinating characters we are; they make our human story the intriguing plot that it is. Embracing the following conditions of existence can nurture our evolution.

> Only alone do I find my unique path. Only with others do I learn to cooperate, accept and give support, and see the limits of what can be expected from others.
>
> Only in a transitory world do I transcend time for the timeless.
>
> Only in an unpredictable universe do I expend all the effort I can muster.
>
> Only in suffering do I make contact with my inner resources of strength and become compassionate.
>
> Only in a world in which I may be powerless over injustice do I strive for justice in any ways I can achieve it.
>
> Only when I face things too big for my level of strength do I open to grace and thereby stretch my powers.

The givens of life have been variously referred to as "Adam's curse," the will of God, or simply the human condition. They are universal in that no one is exempt from them or immune to them, nor can any one of them be repealed. We individuals are not victims of these conditions; they are simply the human reality. To contemplate this fact is to ask oneself, "Am I willing to share the confusion and pain of my fellow human beings? Can I face life, as E. M. Forster writes in *Howard's End,* "not as a victim or a fanatic but as a seafarer who can greet with an equal eye the deep he is entering and the shore that he must leave"?

In reality, these givens are precisely what it takes for us to be and become who we are. Confounding realities like aloneness, the suffering of the just, the pain required for growth, etc., cease to be questions when our spirituality is founded on a stabilizing trust in the aptness of these conditions for our evolution. Such confidence is the trusty horse on which we ride out the chaotic times in life. The conditions of existence are meant to be like weather conditions. If I live in a house with a sturdy roof, walls, and a foundation, I can let the storms come and I still abide safely. "Though the seas threaten, they are merciful," writes Shakespeare in *The Tempest*.

The conditions of our existence are assisting forces on the path to our destiny. Each is a synchronicity since each is connected to a discovery: without aloneness, I never would have found the vast inner world of wisdom and healing power within me. If what I see and desire were not transitory, I never would have looked beyond or through the persons and things in my life to contact the transcendent. If all were predictable, my eyes would never be opened by surprises, by the unexpected, by serendipity. The element of surprise in synchronicity is the Dionysian spirit, granting us access to a lively energy that transcends the narrow promises of orderly logic. Without suffering, I would never have found my inner resources, never have felt the grief that gives me depth and character, never have opened my heart to compassion. If things were always fair, I would have no motivation to recognize and handle the shadow in myself and others in creative ways. This is how the givens of life can be ingredients of wholeness and gifts of grace.

It is synchronicity that we have healthy responses in us that can match the very conditions with which we are confronted. We have tears to process our grief and smiles to express our merriment. We have inner sources and outer resources of nurturance to deal with loneliness, capacities for acceptance and for changing, and bodies capable of handling varying moods in ourselves and in others. We have resources to turn to when we cannot handle conditions and crises, and we can even fall apart and reassemble someday.

We may wish there were a savior who would release us from the harsh exigencies of our humanity. But any savior figure who has appeared has submitted to the conditions, not abrogated them. We cannot expect an interventionist God, though we can trust that there will be special times in which we feel held or protected by kindly forces as we face our calamities. Holocaust survivor Elie Wiesel says, "There is no messiah but there are messianic moments when we choose to care and to humanize our destiny." We are messiahs to ourselves and to the world when we care, and others are messiahs to us when they care.

Religion is designed to respond to the givens of existence. There is consolation in the belief that the immediate, existential experience is not the whole reality. Religion can be used to shield us from the full brunt of life's conditions, promising repeal in this life or the next. An adult with faith trusts a divine providence and protection not as a shield from life's conditions. He trusts that no matter what may happen, he will still be surrounded with grace, especially the grace to love. This is how divine providence is real. A person of faith has to ask himself if he seeks the consolations of God or the God of all consolation who often does not console but allows him to face the givens baldly and boldly.

Buddhism suggests a practice of "joyful participation in the sorrows of the world." The Bhagavad Gita recommends that we become "the same in suffering and joy, content always." Christ suggests trust in his Heart as source of consolation. Saint Ignatius of Loyola advocates that the tidal laws of our life be greeted with "holy indifference"—not stoic indifference but acceptant detachment. Goethe remarks: "As long as you have not grasped that you have to die to grow, you are a troubled guest on the dark earth." Mircea Eliade adds, in speaking of the hero: "The law of life lives in him with his unreserved consent." Similarly, Hamlet calls Horatio "a man whom fortune's buffets or rewards hath taken with equal thanks." Thus Shakespeare proposes gratitude in the face of life's givens. Jung also proposes an etiquette when facing life's conditions. They can be embraced with "an unconditional Yes to that which is, without subjective protests, an acceptance of the conditions of existence . . . an acceptance of my own nature as I happen to be."

We seem so often to be fearing and avoiding the very conditions that give us sensitivity and character. Have we forgotten that Demeter, goddess of life on earth, and Persephone, married to Death, are mother and daughter? They are metaphors for life and death united in one cyclic process. Have we lost sight of the myth of the wounded healer, the one who bears endings, grief, and calamity and thereby brings integration and serenity?

Our ego experiences life through the cycles of fear and craving instead of the cycles of letting go and going on. In fact, our lifelong attachment to the drama of fear and grasping is what endorses the belief in ego as a refuge. Once we see this, we may be ready for a liberating shift. We begin by exposing the way we relate to life predicaments through ego-reinforcing habits that simply reconfirm us in fear and desire. Attachment to such drama is not wrong or sinful. It is an error, since nothing can be truly held onto in this transitory existence. That inclination in us to such a sad error can lead to compassion for ourselves, another pathway toward liberation from ego.

Once we realize that all is impermanent, there is nothing to grasp, cling to, or control, and there is no one to do the clinging. If all things are impermanent, then so is the ego that desires them. "I let go of my insistence on control and entitlement. I drop all attempts to uphold my ego. I stop using people or things to end my loneliness. I give up being so possessive in my relationships. I give up my defending of my ego territory in favor of opening myself to the spacious territory of love, wisdom, and healing." This is how we renounce the premises of ego and enter more stately mansions.

There is an intriguing Zen response to the condition of impermanence. Two terms are used. *Danken* is accepting that all is impermanent so accumulation is useless. *Joken* is maintaining our commitment to work toward goals of health and welfare anyway. Each of these alone is one-sided. To accept impermanence as a condition as well as the legitimacy of goal orientation is the Middle Way of Buddhism: "I endure and overcome with no attempt to resolve. I am defenseless against life's surprises and simultaneously resourceful in the face of them." This combination of defenselessness and resourcefulness is the basis of freedom from fear. They are alternate words for Yes.

Our modern myth, based on fear and denial of life's givens, seeks to extinguish necessary decay by health fads and cosmetic interventions. Our movies attempt to salve us with happy endings in which good triumphs over evil and the wicked are punished. We sometimes have enlisted the courts to compensate our every loss, even the ones we are accountable for. We thus may use the law to indemnify our losses so that we will not have to grieve over them.

Every person, place, and thing that becomes an object of attachment is uncannily designed to teach us the lesson/given of impermanence and deficiency. This is the coincidence of transitory things in a world of grasping hands and clinging hearts. A psychological synchronicity comes to our aid and allows our disappointments to be integrated with our built-in ability to grieve and let go. There is also synchronicity in the spiritual path of egolessness in that it offers us the skillful means to avoid becoming attached in the first place.

A practice is to leave our roses in the vase long after they are withered. Learning to appreciate each phase of a flower's life—from bud to death—is a way of expanding our sense of impermanence to acknowledge the beauty in each of its changes rather than only in one.

How What Happens Helps

One of the conditions of existence is that sometimes we will be faced with more than we can bear. There is a capacity in the human psyche to handle the conditions of its existence, just as animals have innate capacities and instincts to deal with their conditions. Our innate capacities can be developed as programs of skill to deal with aloneness, unpredictability, unfairness, transitoriness, suffering, etc. This is the sense in which we can handle things: always one day at a time. We do notice times, however, when we cannot handle what happens and are devastated by it. We can fall apart in those moments and still trust that eventually we will reconstruct our fragmented pieces and go on. The grace will be about that and about an assurance that our capacity to love will not be destroyed no matter what. That single certainty is the foundation of hope, what Emily Dickinson calls "the thing with feathers—that perches in the soul."

Life is continually baffling us with its contradictions, and we can be overwhelmed and demoralized by them or we can allow them to pass through us with equipoise. The unconditional Yes that allows us to be defense-less releases our lively energy that makes us resource-full. Such a yes is the antidote to fear. This combination of letting go and taking hold frees us from possession by the givens and renders us able to relate to them. The givens of human existence are not inconveniences to be put up with but the most appropriate and precise conditions for the achievement of our highest goal. They are the steps we tread to transformation. They are a path, like synchronicity itself, to the release of unconditional love, wisdom, and the power to heal ourselves and others. Without these blows and challenges, we would be empty Pollyannas in a superficial world.

To keep us on our toes and to maintain homeostasis, events occur that shake us up or cool us down. Everything that happens to us, every person who comes along in our lives, every success, failure, betrayal, or loyalty is meant not to debilitate us but to empower us. Each is synchronicity when it is noticed as a part of our growth. Only through a variety of experiences of all of life's options can we reach our potential for fulfillment and personal power. We can work with this elegantly or be dragged to it kicking and screaming.

The Roman poet Terence writes, "Nothing human is alien from me." To be human is to be susceptible to all the conditions of existence and not in control of any of them. Healthy people have made peace with that. We cannot be in full control, but we can have a program, a plan, a technology to deal with the things that happen to us. It is wise and necessary to have a ready resource to meet our predicaments in the course of life. Experiences and crises that come to us in synchronous ways are meant to deepen us and to show us our path. When we have no program, we lose those options. We have safe passage but no threshold to cross. We survive but may fail to evolve.

For example, earthquakes show us how little in control we are. Yet, there are earthquake safety rules we can follow. This is the program that gives some measure of control to our response so that we can get through it with the least amount of damage. It is remarkable to notice that the old advice on earthquake safety was to tense against it in a doorway. Now the recommendation is to go with the movement, to roll in the hallway, our bodies balled up to avoid too much impact. This is the wisdom of combining control and surrender, a wisdom gained when control is given up by the adult ego as a child gives up baby toys for more challenging ones.

We sometimes face the crisis of indecision. Nothing is so discouraging as being so stymied or stuck in dilemmas that no decision seems possible. But the stuckness can be configured as the pause, the "mysterious pass through the apparently impenetrable mountains" described in the Tao. Then we might say, "I acknowledge this stuckness as synchronicity, a coincidence of between being stopped beyond my control and getting an opportunity for the practice of pausing. What has happened to me is becoming a skillful means for spiritual progress. I am not stuck but released when I go willingly into this gap. I am released from my ego's dualisms. As I trust this space and relax into it, something will automatically change and I will know my next step with intuitive ease. Inner space is simply my potential. As I enter the pause, the mysterious pass in the lost hills, all the old habitual conceptions of myself disappear. In their silent place only the divine light remains, the light that I have always and already been. This divinity is the fully activated potential of myself. God or Buddha-mind are the archetypes of this profound awakening to my true identity, a space that is ever more alight. The crisis of 'no way to decide' turns out to be a luminous space. I reach it not by attempting to fill it but by pausing inside it so it can become a pass."

Our life is not a sequence of events with no purpose. It is an intelligible whole that describes our origin, our destiny, and our response to the opportunities and obstacles along our path. Synchronicity makes life's conditions a series of significant moments and transitions. Transformation happens to us by our handling of the givens of life. The whole narrative of our life is then an integral experience of movement from darkness to light, from confusion to clarity, from isolation to communion.

What is the meaning of life in the biological sense? The history of evolution seems to suggest a meaning of progress in consciousness.

What is the meaning of life in the sense of a lifetime? The universal mythic theme seems to revolve around a heroic journey. Meaningfulness is a phenomenon of movement in both cases.

When we open to the larger meaning of our lifetime and see it as a contribution to the collective human journey, we are living in the heart of the universe. When we appreciate the graces that come to us to make this happen and the love that wants us to find ourselves, we are joyously alive. The journey has three stages: departure, struggle, and return with gifts.

The journey from birth to a sense of a coherent self begins in an undifferentiated unity. This is a healthy symbiosis with our mother. Soon we become differentiated; we explore and affirm our individuality. We do this as we separate from dependency on our parents. This is the hero's departure from comforts. This phase shows how estrangement is in the origin of our self-consciousness. As we become individuated, we emerge into the world to deal with life's conditions and givens. This is the hero's struggle phase. We find the strength, through ruptures, to face challenges and to mend divisions. We are now doing the work of Christ and Buddha. Reconciliation is thus a part of our spiritual maturation. It is the gift we give to those around us, the final victory of the returning hero.

> At the center of the universe is a loving heart that continues to beat and that wants the best for every person. Anything that we can do to help foster the intellect, spirit, and emotional growth of our fellow human beings is our job. Those of us who have this particular vision must continue against all odds. Life is for service.
>
> —FRED ROGERS (A.K.A. "MISTER ROGERS")

USING THE TOOLS

There are many examples of programs we can have in place when facing our life predicaments. These are the tools of the healthy ego.

Each provides a way of *going on*. These are strategies to face the givens of our lives—something we are glad to do once we trust them as synchronously connected to our growth.

None of these programs includes drugs, food, sex, or other compulsions. None of them resorts to silver-lining consolations that are not true and that contradict the conditions of existence. Examples of such consolations are: "Well, I always did my best." No one always did her best throughout her life, nor is that to be expected. "Things will always work out for the best." Things will not always work out for the best, as wars and genocides have shown. "It is karma." This is a deterministic use of the concept of karma that may serve to excuse us from adult responsibility for our actions. "God will provide." Provision for human needs will not always happen, as starving children learn each day. We have to provide for ourselves—and others—in many ways.

Healthy tools for facing life predicaments may include the following:

1. When I am afraid, I can admit my fear, allow myself to feel it fully, and then act as if the fear could not stop me. The more I relax into reality rather than run from it, the more do the fears—that have been my unwelcome companions all my life—finally let me go.

2. If I am angry, I can express it responsibly and directly to the person involved without blame or violence.

3. If I am passive in my interactions with others, I can learn to be assertive and to stand my ground without becoming aggressive.

4. When I suddenly feel fragmented and depressed because my life seems to have been a waste, I can imagine a kindly, avuncular voice inside that says, "It's not so bad as I am making it out to be. Let me look at all I have done, both positive and negative. I made some mistakes, but everyone does. What matters is that I have gone on and know better now. Give myself some credit!"

5. In the void—the black hole of panic in which nothing works and our lively energy is on hold—we can simply stay in the suspense, without having to do anything. We can let it be and listen to its eerie silence until we feel an impetus to move in some new direction. The timing is never from ego but from the Self's calendar of synchronicities.

6. If I feel guilty, I can make amends and resolve to change my behavior for the future.

7. If someone says something cruel to me, I may be tempted to resort to the ego's program of retaliation. Instead, I can declare to the other how hurt I am to hear that and how it is unacceptable to me to be spoken to in that way. When the ego voice within says, "I should have come back at him with . . . " I can acknowledge that as the indignant ego, and respond with an affirmation: "I let go of the need to retaliate. I choose to handle things creatively and strongly but kindly too." The work is to clear away all the neurotic ego's programs from our modus operandi and to replace them with loving and yet assertive ones.

8. If I am betrayed by a partner, I can resort to the ego's armory and defend myself against further hurts by putting up a wall against future relationships. Such self-defense walls me in. On that wall, the scared ego has scratched its self-defeating graffiti: "You cannot trust men/women. They will always disappoint you. You cannot handle the normal give-and-take of relationship with all its potential for pain. Stay away from all future relationships." I may believe these bitter verdicts and thus abandon myself. Suddenly, passion goes out of my life, as do my chances for pleasure and fulfillment.

It is stressful to maintain a repression of the natural human instinct to bond. Wholeness means giving free rein to all our instincts and susceptibilities. Healthy people are willing to love again, ready to risk the same disasters they faced before, because they have found a resource for future reference. Griefwork is the program for dealing with betrayal and abandonment. Those who have grieved and let go will choose new partners more wisely and be more psychologically nimble in their grieving the next parting, if that were to occur.

9. Sometimes we will have face something that is too big for us to handle alone. Then our program is to seek help. If I have a cut on my finger, I can use the program of first aid that I have lined up for just such emergencies, peroxide and Band-Aids close at hand. If I cut an artery, I will have to go for help to the hospital, where the doctor will provide the necessary technology of suturing me. Likewise, in a psychological crisis, I may need to consult a therapist to help me design a program that meets my needs with a healthy resource. Becoming healthy does not mean that painful things no longer happen to us but that we now have ways of handling whatever may happen.

10. The given of injustice may make us wonder why the innocent suffer. But this presumes that suffering is a punishment for evil. In the world of the loving Self, there is no punishment, only consequences and opportunities for transformation. To wish that the wicked will suffer is ego-vengeful. To work for their transformation is loving. How have I responded to the evil done to me? What do I feel about punishment, including prison and capital punishment? Do I have a heart that feels sadness for both the victim and the perpetrator? How can I work toward an alternative to the violence of punishment? Is my God an extension of the male punitive ego? Am I creating hell on earth or heaven on earth?

11. In Buddhism, there are the eight worldly concerns that challenge our equanimity. These are four pairs of cravings/fears, and to find a path through the center of each set of these dualisms is to be liberated from ego's excessive desire for positive experiences and terror of negative ones: gain and loss, fame and infamy, praise and blame, pleasure and pain. Where do I stand? How can I stand with equipoise and equanimity?

12. Recite this declaration and notice what you feel about it: "It is only when I have the courage to face things as they are, without any self deception or illusion, that a light will shine from events, and a path to contentment will open for me. Since all predicaments teach and awaken me, I can be grateful to them all. I do not push my predicament away; I find a way to lean on it. I choose to have no escape hatch. My Yes is unconditional."

Bring loving-kindness to your practice by adding: "By the power and truth of this predicament, may all beings have happiness and be free of fear and craving. May I never destroy anyone's happiness. May all people keep choosing the path of peace and cherish all that lives as holy. Everything that happens to me is from a sacred heart, a light that will not go out, something unfolding and enfolding. I say Yes to the path with heart."

13. Here is a summary model for healthy, functional responses to the conditions of existence. What can I install into my lifestyle to make these responses happen more and more?

Deal with:	By:
Aloneness	Building a support system
Transitoriness	Letting go
Unpredictability	Trusting synchronicity
Suffering	Accepting what cannot be changed, changing what can be changed
Unfairness	Accepting what cannot be changed, changing what can be changed

Finally, we can admit that even the healthiest ego may be powerless to effect certain changes in the psyche. No psychological program works to make an arrogant ego surrender easily. On its own the ego cannot "turn the other cheek," love or forgive unconditionally, or give itself away in compassionate generosity. These are callings from a spiritual source that not everyone will hear. They hearken from the world of the Self where grace presides. How ironic—and humbling—that we cannot release what is best in us on our own. How fortunate that graces abound.

14. The hero leaves where he is, goes through many struggles, and meets up with assisting and afflicting forces, and finally finds a treasure that he brings back home. Here is a model in which we can locate ourselves in those same three phases of life's journey in our past, present, and future. Where are you, and what are the synchronicities that are coming to meet you?

I am where I have been for awhile.

Something happens that challenges me to change or go.

I cross a threshold to embark on something new.

I meet up with afflicting forces, am wounded in many ways, even possibly become immobilized.

I am visited by assisting forces who rescue me or give me a special grace to break through my stuckness or my injuries.

I find something out or find something of great value not by effort but as a gift of grace.

I bring this gift back to where I began, willing to share it freely and generously.

Some understand me and some do not. Some accept my gifts and some refuse. I do not force, nor do I give up. I keep sharing my gifts in any way I can.

I rest in the light of equanimity and let it through me continually.

CRISIS

A Given and a Spur

A friend rejects us. A partner leaves us. A company fires us. A loved one unexpectedly dies. We are devastated and at a loss as to what to do about these givens that have come our way. In such crises we are frightened as well as grief stricken. We are finding out that our sources of security had no real foundation. Meister Eckhart said, "Everything is meant to be lost that the soul may stand in unhampered nothingness." A crisis leads to a discarding. But of what? Only of the illusions, disguises, and masks that we were relying on to establish our identity. The true Self can emerge only from the surrender of the deluded ego.

An ego crisis is weathered successfully when we can fall apart and then trust that we will reassemble. Our trust is based on the fact that the healthy ego has the skill of restoration. This is being transformed by pain. The pain has been useless if we get back in full control when all the signals say, "Let it happen." Jung referred to this as "the regressive restoration of persona." It is putting the old mask back on. It is a refusal to "stand in unhampered nothingness," the only launching pad for a new way of living.

Creation myths begin with chaos. Chaos is the given/condition for something new to emerge. The meaningful connection is synchronicity. A personal crisis is a microcosm of the primordial chaos and the synchronous prerequisite for creative possibilities. When things become topsy-turvy in our life, something is ready to be born in us. We may ask, "Why me?" *Why* is from the vocabulary of intellect and reason. Crisis does not hearken to us from that realm. It transcends and defies the rational. It is the paradox of a chaos that *necessarily* precedes a new creation. Logic and making sense of things are usually impossible to achieve in crisis. Pausing is the proper etiquette, brooding over the troubled waters, not draining them away.

Crisis usually represents a confrontation or an argument with one or more of the conditions of existence. Crisis is a challenge to change. To change is to locate a new level of strength in ourselves and to act in accord with it; to stay unchanged is to regress. There is no middle ground of safety. This is why in a crisis, we enter the void. We see how much of our security was a prop meant to uphold a shaky ego. In crisis, we feel powerless to maintain the old comfortable structures. We are then forced to marshal our strengths and move into something new. Perhaps a grace comes our way; we find strength we did not think we had. We live through the crisis; we are still standing after the storm. What threatens us with breakdown leads to breakthrough. A paradox has appeared; without props, we still stand. Emily Dickinson uses this same metaphor:

> The props assist the House
> Until the House is built,
> And then the props withdraw—
> And adequate, erect,
> The House supports itself;
> Ceasing to recollect
> The Auger and the Carpenter—
> Just such a retrospect
> Hath the perfected Life,
> A past of Plank and Nail,
> And slowness,—then the Scaffolds drop—
> Affirming it a Soul.

Occasionally, the little rain that must fall into every life becomes a hurricane. A nonstop series of disasters occurs that lays us low or casts us into the void. This puts too much pressure on our capacity to handle things since it is happening too fast for the "one day at a time" approach. There is no power that is seeing to it that this will not happen to *me*. One of the conditions of existence is that anything can happen to anyone. It is normal to break down under such pressure and then reconstitute later. Suicide or despair are the rejection of this possibility.

In a breakdown, it is normal to experience runaway feelings. Anger may keep flaring up uncontrollably; sadness may lead to crying jags; fear may lead us to be phobic about almost everything and even superstitious or paranoid. Obsessive thoughts may plague us. All of these are normal when they are phase appropriate; they are characteristic of the first-blush reaction to overwhelming crisis. When we are basically functional, they end as we move toward acceptance and resolution. In a neurotic character structure, the inappropriate feelings, behavior, and thoughts hang on indefinitely.

Traumatic events and crises are familiar. Most of us have felt them since childhood or even infancy. They have imprinted us with stress, anxiety, and uneasiness that manifest in our bodies, in our sense of who we are, in our way of moving, in our beliefs about our masculinity or femininity, in the way we relate, and even in our physical shape and health. We designed the strategies of a lifetime from the impact of crises and injuries.

Our work is to untangle and undo the knots we tied. That task, when handled conscientiously and successfully, makes us kinder to others and certainly less likely to inflict the same hurts on them. Suffering softens us when we allow it, bear it, and then move on. The allowing is letting go of control. The bearing is letting go of seeking an escape. The moving on is not becoming stuck in being a victim. We then see the crisis as not quite so bad. The friendlier we become to ourselves, the friendlier will our predicament look to us.

In a crisis, we may feel forsaken. This forsakenness is a sense of a withdrawal of our assisting forces. Is the message coming through to us that it's time to take a break from looking outside? Can we experience the void inside ourselves and in our world? Can we drop into the spaciousness of it, simply sitting as fair and alert witnesses of the shambles around us? We might thereby contact our immanence because of our forsakenness. We might find transcendence because of limitation. Negatives are necessary in an equation if one is to find the positives on the other side.

In a crisis, our ego often fails us. A crisis is thus an opportunity for a breakthrough of the archetypal world into the ego's inflated opinion of itself. Synchronicity is more observable when the ego is not in the way since archetypes constellate more strongly as our ego deflates. Has the crisis happened for this reason? John 6:19 states, "The wind was strong and the sea was rough . . . when they saw Jesus walking on the water toward their boat."

A crisis in the hero's journey is meant to precipitate a move. Why the tornado in *The Wizard of Oz*? Dorothy would not have gone otherwise. She tried to leave on her own but was easily persuaded to return, her journey interrupted before it began. Along comes the crisis, the painful event beyond her control that is in fact the grace that hurls her into her destiny. A crisis can be the spur of the moment, the initiatory pain that leads us out, the synchronicity of an unwanted event and challenge to evolve.

Crisis makes for tragedy; transformation happens in comedy. To see the humor of a critical event is a path toward working it through. Comedy, like spirituality, thrives on contrast and then unites opposites. This may be why so many comedies end with a wedding! Humor is often predicated on the ego getting its comeuppance. In comedy, everything is mixed up: decorum and license, prince and pauper, accord and discord, order and disorder, male and female, fantasy and reality. Boundaries and identities are tested and stretched. In the comic sense of things, tension is bearable, as in sports, which comfortably combine tension and enjoyment. The sense of humor in comedy defies law and logic. It is at ease with the crossover of the conceptual to the imaginative, as Hermia indicates in Shakespeare's *A Midsummer Night's Dream:* "Methinks I see these things with parted eyes, when everything seems double." Comedy keeps the promise that in time things will work out, that miracles can happen just in time. In tragedy, it is always too late. In the tragic outcome, the chance for amends is irretrievably lost. In comedy, all is forgiven and the largesse of this forgiveness leads to amendment. As Puck says in *A Midsummer Night's Dream,* "If you pardon, we will mend." Forgiving has the power to induce contrition in the one forgiven.

DIVING IN

A crisis helps us face something about ourselves that we have been overlooking. If we look carefully, we might see that all the crises and issues of our lives go back to a central fear. For example, we may believe that vulnerability will lead to being dropped, that we must always expect the worst, that a catastrophe has always been waiting for us. We can resolve that fear by choosing to *dive*. There is an ancient archetypal dimension to this theme, and it helps us to know more about daring to free ourselves from fear. In pagan times, a dive was considered a conscious baptism, a plunge of the ego into the waters that dissolve it. Diving is a symbol of daring the death of the ego and of its frantic clinging to fear and desire. To resurface from the water is to be reborn in the likeness of the Self, that is, purified of attachment. A Hindu scripture says that the sea dissolves our name, that is, our exclusive identification with ego.

A leap is a metaphor for the combination of two opposites, fear of risk and surrender to it. Diving into our pain and predicament represents a readiness for total letting go—without having to be pushed. It is heroic because it is voluntary. Diving off a very high cliff was a sacrament in ancient Greece and Turkey. This was the order of the rite: First a priest recited myths about heroes and their feats. This made the ancestral heroes present as assisting forces and encouraging advocates to the diver. An intoxicating herb was then given to the diver to make it easier to dare the leap into the waters awaiting him. The attending women shouted words of encouragement. The young man then dove off the cliff. His life flashed before him as he sailed through the air, as if it were being reviewed for the last time and then ended in its former way. The gods' grace supported him, and he emerged reborn from the waters to the cheers of the people.

Diving also became associated with proofs of daring or caring. Pliny says that Sappho, an excellent diver, dove from a cliff in Lesbos "to transcend earthly love." Throughout history, from China to New England, the ritual plunge became a judicial ordeal to prove one's innocence or one's favor with God. Christian baptism, based on Judaic tradition, is a plunge into the waters that bring about the death of the old Adam (ego) and rebirth as a new Christ (Self) in the human soul. It is a sacrament in that it is a correlation of a ritual and a grace, an act with a result that matches it, hence synchronicity.

In the Greek rite, the women who stood on the sidelines and encouraged the men to dive portray an archetypal role of the feminine: to help drown the male ego. The Sirens, Lorelei, and mermaids are personifications of this seduction into dissolution—a role women have played archetypally for centuries. Any ordinary guy today has noticed it happening in his relationship with women too. In our relationships, we may be willing to live together, to love, to be faithful. Are we willing to risk this other plunge into the dissolving of our ego? If only we trusted that when ego goes, all our fears go with it. Fear dives in, but it is courageous love that climbs out.

> If there is a fear of falling, the only safety is in deliberately jumping.
>
> —CARL JUNG

A MINDFUL PRACTICE

Sit comfortably with your eyes closed and with your cupped hands in your lap, paying attention to your breathing. Notice your breathing in, breathing out, and the little gap between the breaths. That momentary stillness is the spaciousness of no-mind, freedom from the ego's storylines of fear and attachment. Rest in it. If thoughts interrupt, simply label them as thoughts and return to awareness of your breathing.

Form an image of your present crisis, problem, or concern and imagine that you are holding it in your cupped hands in the form of a ball. Notice whether you chose the image of a bowling ball, golf ball, etc. Acknowledge it as yours. Notice how heavily your problem ball weighs and let your hands drop farther down if appropriate. Now imagine that the ball is covered with five layers, each of which you will examine and then shed:

The first layer is that of fear. What is scary about this problem and how are you holding onto the fear or being stopped or pushed by it? Once you are aware of your felt sense of this fear, imagine that you are peeling it away from your problem ball and dropping it aside. You affirm: "I let go of the need to fear this."

In each of these layers, to say "I let go" simply means "I picture what it would be like to let go of this layer." You do not have to wait till you feel you truly have let go of it. This part of the exercise is imagistic and hopefully leads to a sense that "it can happen."

The second layer is that of control. How invested are you in controlling the outcome of this problem, and how are you trying to maintain control of others around you? Once you are aware of your felt sense of this need/compulsion to control, imagine that you are peeling it away from your problem ball and dropping it aside. You affirm: "I let go of the need to control this."

The third layer is that of blame. How are you blaming this problem on someone else? Once you are aware of your felt sense of this blaming, imagine that you are peeling it away from your problem ball and dropping it aside. You affirm: "I let go of the need to blame anyone for this."

The fourth layer is that of shame. How are you feeling shame or guilt about having this problem? Once you are aware of your felt sense of this self-recrimination, imagine that you are peeling it away from your problem ball and dropping it aside. You affirm: "I let go of the need to feel ashamed of this."

The fifth layer is that of the need to get in control and fix the problem. How are you letting your serenity become dependent upon whether you can bring everything back to normal? Once you are aware of your felt sense of this burdensome task, imagine that you are peeling it away from your problem ball and dropping it aside. You affirm: "I let go of the need to fix this."

Return your attention to your breathing, noticing the gaps between your breaths as well as the breaths themselves. Notice if the ball feels lighter. Has it become as light as a ping-pong ball? Ask yourself what is left of the original problem now that it is shorn of the five layers of ego. Can it now be pure space, like the gap between your breaths, like what is in a ping-pong ball?

Now touch the earth with your cupped hands and lift them over the crown of your head as you open them and let go of what is left of the problem in a gesture of offering and releasing. Open your eyes and give thanks to the first thing you see in nature. Support from nature was the experience of grace for Buddha, who touched the earth as his witness and who gazed with thanks at the Bodhi tree for seven days in thanksgiving for being enlightened under it.

You are now the fair and alert witness within and outside your problem. Something has been born that sits safely in the center of and yet also beyond the entanglements of your struggle. Free of dualisms, neither stoic nor stuck, you can observe conflict with feeling and yet with focus on its pure meaning and spiritual challenge. This is attention to both the figure and ground of whatever faces you. Nothing really has to be complicated or confused. The embroideries of ego create those conditions. We are so used to being ruled by them, we think they are insurmountable.

You can locate the simplicity and lightness of your being through mindful practices like the one above. You can freely go with the flow of your life and, at the same time, be able to hearken back to a reliable still point that is impervious to the ups and downs of daily dramas. This still point *is* oneness, the ultimate spaciousness behind all the appearances of things and behind all the layerings of ego. The stillness may only last for a moment but it is delicious enough to keep you coming back for more, and it is only a breath away. Any issue granted this kind of egoless attention becomes a silence richer than words and leads to surprises.

We have an inner inclination—even an urgency—to be open to what is and to attune to reality as it is. The inhibiting mind wants to dress up reality in accord with its own fears and desires. These are attempts to protect our opening self from feelings, especially hurt and disappointment. Mindfulness means simply noticing our feelings and paying attention to them rather than seeking a refuge in serenity or disregard. Mindfulness meditation is visiting the mind as a witness, not escaping it as a prisoner. It is not dissociation from our feelings but disidentifying with their possessive power over us. We do this, paradoxically, by experiencing them and then stepping into what comes next. We never have to doubt that we know how to open to this process. We do not have to try to open; we are always and already there. The work is to catch ourselves at closing and gently reopen.

Write a poem or prayer about this potential and actual power in yourself.

We can practice recontextualizing and thereby transforming the challenging life conditions that we are presented with. For example, when tragedy strikes in my life, I am tempted to ask, "What did I do to deserve this?" This is a normal guilt reaction with roots in childhood superstition. An adult—and more highly evolved—spiritual alternative is now presented to me: "*This is not about what I did. This is about what I am called to be.*" This way of configuring crisis is in keeping with the relationship between synchronicity and destiny. Everything that happens is about how I am called to be all that I can be, not about how bad I was or how victimized I am. How have the tragedies and crises in my life opened the door to new vistas, helped me find my own truth, led me to show more love, and made me more compassionate toward and understanding of others? When I focus on these questions, I make what has happened workable in the ongoing unfolding of my heroic story.

I now affirm that I can tolerate my emotional reactions without being overwhelmed by them. I sometimes feel myself collapsing under the weight of my concerns or problems. I can decide to hold my disintegration rather than try to escape from it or fix it. I can hold my terrifying feelings as I hold a child with a terrifying nightmare. Simply by holding and cradling him, I help him regain his reason and be soothed. I can hold myself that way, and thereby reconstitute myself. I can hold my own disintegration till it becomes integrated. The belief that restitution will follow disruption leads to a sense of trust in the universe and in the cohesive strength within me. Feelings then become signs of lively tides, not of tidal waves. I am ready to dive.

I say to myself (and/or my partner):

> You can be broken down, and I will hold and love you that way.
> You can fall apart, and I will hold and love you that way.

You can have nothing to offer for now, and I will hold and
love you that way.

You can be at your lowest ebb, and I will hold and love you
that way.

You can be depressed, contorted, wounded, or distraught,
and I will hold and love you that way.

I will do this with no insistence that you be fixed. I can accommodate a you that breaks down and is not available
for my needs for the time being.

In quantum physics, the "principle of indeterminacy" refers to the
fact that chance and unpredictability meet at the very heart of matter. Evolution brings order to this chaos, but the chaos remains
nonetheless. Our personal work is to contain just such opposites
within ourselves. This means allowing crises to unfold and doing all
we can to evoke harmony from them. This is welcoming what enters
our world and waving good-bye to what wants to go. Perfect joy happens when we no longer oppose what is.

Answer these questions in your journal: What is chaotic in my
life? How can I allow the chaos? How can I bring harmony and order
to it? What is ready to be said good-bye to? What is ready to be wel-
comed? What am I holding out against? What wants to happen? What
are the conditions of my existence now? How am I facing them?
What is love's best chance in any of this?

Pip loved life and all life's peaceable securities, so that the
panic-striking business in which he had somehow unaccount-
ably become entrapped, had most sadly burned his brightness; though, as ere long would be seen, what was thus
temporarily subdued in him, in the end was destined to be
luridly illumined by strange wild fires, that fictitiously
showed him off to ten times the natural lustre with which
in his native Tolland County in Connecticut, he had once
enlivened many a fiddler's frolic on the green; and at

melodious even-tide, with his gay ha-ha! had turned the round horizon into one star-belled tambourine.

—HERMAN MELVILLE, *Moby Dick*

GUIDES WHO COME TO WAVE US ON

Although I showed you the path to liberation, you must walk it alone.

—GAUTAMA BUDDHA

The hero acknowledges that his own capacities and efforts are inadequate to the full requirements of his task. He consults the archetype of wisdom in the form of a trusted advisor. This emerges from the hero's spiritual yearning to hear a numinous voice, to make contact with the infinite, to ask for the grace that takes him beyond the limitations of his own knowledge and powers. It is not about seeking answers to mundane questions. It is an acknowledgment that he will always have to look beyond himself to find himself.

Assisting forces continually appear in history and in our quotidian life. They take many forms: people, writings, animals, etc. Scriptures like the Vedas, the Bible, the Koran, etc. are examples of guides. They are limitless wisdom submitting to the limits of time and space, a kind of incarnation. The teachings mirror the wisdom of the inner Self, which is why they are recognizable as wise. Since this is so, the teachings hail to us from beginnings of humanity. A teacher or guru is legitimate as a channel because he is in a line of succession to that beginning. For a true teacher, the teachings are the teacher.

A person who is a true guide has characteristics like these:

- He asks for respectful attention, not blind obedience.
- He is an escort to our unique destiny and does not require that we follow his. To honor such a guide evokes his power to show us the path, protect us, and even give us the grace of an impetus from which there is no turning back.

- A valid guide always leads us back to ourselves and the riches within us. He does not want to be clung to as a source, but only be attended to as a temporary channel. He empowers us to find the power in ourselves. Buddha uses the analogy of the raft for his teachings. A raft is provisional; it works to get us across the river but then it is meant to be left behind so that we can walk unencumbered through our own jungle. The best teachings/teacher are those we can leave safely at the threshold of what comes next for us on our journey. The raft/teachings bring us to where the journey begins, and then it is our task to enlist new forces from within.

- A guide may also be one who reveals—or challenges—the meaning of the flora and fauna of the path, cryptic messages from the unconscious.

- A true guide never looks for ego-enhancement or asserts his ego over ours. He leads us beyond our own egos because he has already transcended it in himself. He never takes advantage of us physically, emotionally, sexually, financially, or in any other way.

- Our freedom to choose is a indispensable ingredient for our work of opening ourselves to wholeness. A true guide cherishes and is immensely sensitive to that freedom. He offers external supports only as a means of activating our inner resources, not as replacements of them. He wants us to have our own life, not be dependent on him.

In myth and story, the guide is often a stranger, often of another creed or nationality, for example, the dwarfs in Snow White. Another example is in the Hasidic story of the Czech rabbi who dreams of a treasure buried under a bridge. He does not find the treasure there, but a guard in Prague tells his own dream to the rabbi, mockingly saying he saw a treasure in a rabbi's house under the hearth, which is where the rabbi finds it. All we need is here, but we have to go away sometimes to find that out. Note how the guard/guide ridicules the meaningfulness of dreams. Our guide, too, may point by laughing.

As we become friendlier toward bedrock reality, that reality itself appears more and more as the true guide, ever presenting opportunities for initiation. Unadorned reality gives us our best instruction on the path. Our ego's pretensions to sovereignty collapse in the implacable face of this invincible governor. He seems to thwart us over and over—but only to fulfill us once and for all.

> *Alone, alone, all, all alone,*
> *Alone on a wide wide sea!*
> *And never a saint took pity on*
> *My soul in agony. . . .*
> *A thousand thousand slimy things*
> *Lived on; and so did I. . . .*
> *I looked to heaven, and tried to pray;*
> *But or ever a prayer had gusht,*
> *A wicked whisper came, and made*
> *My heart as dry as dust. . . .*
> *The moving Moon went up the sky,*
> *And no where did abide.*
> *Softly she was going up,*
> *And a star or two beside. . . .*
> *Beyond the shadow of the ship,*
> *I watched the water-snakes. . . .*
> *O happy living things! no tongue*
> *Their beauty might declare*
> *A spring of love gushed from my heart,*
> *And I blessed them unaware*
> *Sure my kind saint took pity on me,*
> *And I blessed them unaware.*
> *The self-same moment I could pray*
> *And from my neck so free*
> *The Albatross fell off, and sank*
> *Like lead into the sea.*

Oh sleep! It is a gentle thing,
Beloved from pole to pole!
To Mary Queen the praise be given!
She sent the gentle sleep from Heaven,
That slid into my soul.

— SAMUEL TAYLOR COLERIDGE,
"The Rime of the Ancient Mariner"

In Coleridge's "Rime of the Ancient Mariner," the mariner killed the albatross and brought bad luck upon himself and the crew. He became an afflicting force when every sailor on board is called upon to be an assisting force. The albatross was a bird of good omen that led ships through icy waters. The mariner unconsciously shot down a spiritual guide, a visionary grace that was meant to complement the sailors' ego efforts on their voyage toward wholeness. This is symbolic of the fact that it is in us sometimes to deny and kill the powers that come to help or love or complete us. The mariner has found no way to make up for his misdeed. Death and loneliness reign. He is condemned to wear the lifeless albatross around his neck. He sits alone one night and simply gazes in rapt attention at the sea and its marvelous creatures. He is staying and attending, that is, being mindful. In this effortless moment, the mariner's "kind saint" takes pity on him, and he blesses the creatures he feared before. In the poem, the words "a spring of love gushed," "my kind saint," "unaware," are all ways of showing the effortless and hence egoless nature of the experience. It is pure grace. It happens to and through the mariner, and at that moment "the albatross fell off, and sank like lead into the sea."

We have only to sit and watch the show. Assisting forces come into play; "my kind saint" releases an abundant spring from my heart and frees something from my neck—and through this intervention of grace, healing happens. The mariner is the ego; the kind saint is the Self. They can be good friends when we have lost our way and our egos offer no navigation.

The albatross in the story is crucial to the mariner's awakening. Animals, both in waking and dream life, often serve as guides or as triggers to transformation. Jung said, "When we become more spiritual, an animal appears." Animals may appear in life experience and in dreams, at synchronous times, to accompany or even escort us along our path. Joseph Campbell writes, "Animals are the great shamans and teachers . . . messengers signaling some wonder . . . one's own personal guardian come to bestow its warning and protection."

Animals sometimes appear synchronously when we need information about our path. This is referred to as animal medicine. For example, I absently look out of a high window pondering if it is time to let go of my relationship. Suddenly, out of nowhere a couple of hummingbirds come directly to the window, where they do not ordinarily appear, and seem to be looking at me. This is "hummingbird medicine" that may be saying, "Keep looking at the relationship and give it a little longer!" An eagle feather falls at my feet as I am fearing to take a certain risk. This is "eagle medicine" perhaps encouraging me to boldness. The synchronicity is in the unexpected and unusual placement of the animal, the timeliness of its appearance, and our noticing the precision of the metaphor.

An allegorical guide figure is the shaman. He serves as a mediator between the visible and the invisible worlds. He is a healer and a seer, the central assisting force in a tribal community, a personification of grace. His vocation comes from a tutelary spirit and from its helper-spirits and cannot be refused. The calling often begins with a wound that is mysteriously healed. The shaman undergoes an initiation of harsh suffering or even dismemberment. His survival is then the reenactment of the death-resurrection theme.

The shaman learns the art of traveling easily from the earthly to the heavenly plane. He ascends with humankind's prayers and descends with divine messages. This is a metaphor for the axis of the profane and the sacred in human integration, an image of the ego/Self axis, all synchronous connections. Since the shaman partakes of both the world of appearances and the world of spirit, he can resist mortal pain at will, for example, walk on hot coals or converse freely with divine beings. The shaman is a *sherpa* to the beyond, a guide who knows the itinerary to the immortal world. His ability to fly is the metaphor of this wisdom about higher things. One of the Vedas says, "Those who know have wings!"

The shaman transcends the human condition and the community reveres him and looks to him as an advocate for its survival. Actually, what they feel is nostalgia since everyone had these powers in the archaic past but lost them as the scared and grasping ego gained ascendancy. *The Egyptian Book of the Dead* describes the soul as a falcon that flies away to the primordial garden. The "original fall" is surely from this flying condition.

Rituals rebuild the bridge between heaven and earth, reviving communication with the spirit world and reconciling men and gods. The shaman crosses this bridge, bringing candidates with him once they are ready. The bridge is open "only for an instant." This is the synchronous moment, the *kairos,* the mysterious pass.

These intriguing metaphors describe our own inner capacity to be guided by beings who know how to transcend opposites, to move beyond the limits of senses and sensibility, and to abolish the polarities of time and timelessness. Shamanism is an abiding promise of a passageway between the warring oppositions that the ego thrives on. This is where nature's laws no longer limit us and freedom becomes expansive in ways we never dreamed possible. The shamanic powers are in the Self and become available to us when we build the bridge between it and the healthy ego. We then fly to spiritual heights and transcend the limits of the time-bound world. Synchronicity is the mediator of this, the familiar shamanic advocate that assists us in the passage from dismembered ego to wholeness. This is the genuine passage to our own authentic being with its own flight patterns, its own sighs, and its own visionary moments.

NOTICING ASSISTING FORCES

1. Who are the guides in your life? How are you thanking them? How have you listened or not listened to their

suggestions? Do the people you consider guides fit the criteria outlined above? How do dreams and synchronicities act as guides and shamans for you?

2. Perhaps guidance does not end with death. Enlightened saints and bodhisattvas promised to remain to help us as we struggle on. Their love, wisdom, and healing did not die with them but live on in the treasury from which we draw every moment of every day. Saint John Chrysostom wrote in his hymn to Mary on the day of her ascent from earth to heaven: "You went away, but you never left us!" Express appreciation to the sources of invisible assistance in your life. If there is ever someone you respect who is about to die, consider asking him/her to be your guide from the next plane for the rest of your life. Ask this also of someone already passed over, especially someone who really loved you.

3. How do I rely on my own effort and imagine that it is all there is? How do I kill or have I killed what most I loved or needed? How do I carry the albatross of my past mistakes? What will it take to let it go? How do I welcome my assisting forces? How do I deny them entry?

The terrifying darkness had become complete. . . . Suddenly, my room blazed with an indescribably white light. I was seized with an ecstasy beyond description. . . . I stood upon the summit of a mountain where a great wind blew. A wind not of air but of spirit. In great, clean strength, it blew right through me. Then came the blazing thought, "You are a free man." . . . A great peace stole over me and . . . I became acutely conscious of a Presence which seemed like a veritable sea of living spirit. I lay on the shores of a new world. . . . For the first time, I felt that I really belonged. I knew that I was loved and could love in return.

—BILL WILSON, FOUNDER OF *Alcoholics Anonymous*,
FROM HIS BOOK, *Bill W.: My First Forty Years*

7

Synchronicity in Our Dreams

In dreams, the psyche speaks in images, and gives expression to
instincts which derive from the most primitive level of nature.
Therefore, through the assimilation of unconscious contents,
the momentary life of consciousness can once more be brought
into harmony with the law of nature, from which it all too easily
departs, and we can be led back to the natural law of our own being.
—CARL JUNG

Myths are metaphors for our human potentials. Dreams are mythic
stories that capture our attention, an attention that can lead to healing. Dreams, poetry, and myths all emerge from the same place, the
point of contact between spirit and matter, human and divine, male
and female, personal and transpersonal, ego and Self, death and life.
These are all related as yin to yang, complementarities that are ultimately unities, like breathing in and out. Dreams are the royal road
to and from the unconscious. They reveal our identity, our path, our
next step, what resides in us, what is ready to emerge or evolve.
Each dream speaks to our condition, though in complex ways. Since

dreams thus reflect and presage our life predicaments, they are re-markable examples of synchronicity.

To know who we are is a twofold task. It is first of all to know our deepest wishes and longings as well as our loves and fears. It is also to know the space that opens in us when we go beyond needs, wishes, and fears to expand our love. Dreams show us how to move between one and the other, how to continue our journey toward wholeness. Dreams introduce us not only to parts of ourselves but also to visiting archetypes—innate energies—that may come to free us from the domination of the ego.

Our ego identity is encrusted with habitual ways of seeing our-selves, others, and our life. It is supremely devoid of surprises, full of hackneyed and predictable responses. Our soul identity is free of habits, biases, and orthodoxy. It is full of surprises, full of grace. Within this spiritual identity is a set of accurate, appropriate, and courageous responses to whatever life may bring. Our true Self is a reliable inner repertory of powers. It is like a Swiss army knife with blades for every circumstance that may face us in the unpredictable forest. Dreams come to us from this power place—or rather, space—in us. Our journey is to advance past our ego's entrench-ments long enough to feel a contact with our wholeness.

Dreams are visions from a superior intelligence that points out our ego's blind spots and challenges us to deal with them. Dreams come from a knowledge larger than ego or our I.Q. They tell us what we do not yet know. How ironic that we have minds that are unable to know the deepest truths about ourselves. What we figure out mentally about the meaning of a dream often misses the mark be-cause dreams speak the Self's language to the ego. They are not ego talking to itself. Like angels, dreams are intelligent agents that come to help us. Decisions made on the basis of logic alone betray this soulful voice within us that, thanks to the frequency of our dreams, will not be silent long.

Dreams do not tell us what to do but simply point to what is un-lived in us. This larger intelligence is unconscious and does not em-ploy logic or clear language. The soul is the dream-maker, not the logical mind. According to Jung, the soul is the connecting link between our consciousness and our unconscious. It is made up of images. The unconscious produces images as the body produces T-cells, pictures that tell how psychological and spiritual healing happens and even make it happen.

Dreams and synchronicity work together most conspicuously in what, as we saw above, Jung calls the transcendent function of the psyche: a healing, synthesizing image arises automatically in a dream when we hold our warring tensions rather than side with any one of them. When we hold, rather than attach ourselves to one polarity, opposites combine. For example, we notice that we are overly controlling at times and yet also at times overly submissive. To hold both of these means that we contemplate both of them, make room for them by accepting their equal legitimacy while not feeling constrained to act solely from one or the other. A healing third option arises: I see myself in a dream being gentle and yet still asserting my rights. In this image—and my consequent plan to put it into action—my quandary is resolved. I respect both sides and find a way to show both sides without violating myself or anyone else. This is how chaos becomes cosmos.

The psyche synchronously produces just the image that helps us reconcile our inner oppositions. We face a conscious conflict at the same time as the psyche provides a solution from our unconscious in an image, that is, from our soul. Butterflies were the most common image on the walls of the children's camps in Nazi Germany. What a touching example of the transcendent function of the beleaguered psyche.

Dreams show our conscious ego where it is on its journey, where it has become one-sided, where changes wait to happen. The face we hide in the daylight turns back to us in dreams. What we have excluded, that is, do not believe we can integrate, now demands inclusion since the psyche contains a powerful instinctive directedness. It wants to include, restore, and integrate everything split off by fear and resistance. We fear anything unknown. We resist our dark side full of dangerous impulses and our light side full of grand potentials for good. Synchronously, a dream brings an image that speaks to this condition. A unique meaning is evoked in this unique dream image in our unique life for our unique life purpose.

Dreams come from the divine nucleus of psyche to the orbiting electrons of daily life. When we listen to our dreams, they take us deeper into the fertile terrain of the Self. *Deeper* means a more meaningful and harmonious connection between ego and Self, that is, more soul. To say that dreams have no meaning is like being in a foreign land and believing that the language spoken there is gibberish. At the same time, dreams are not to be taken literally or as giving total information. Sometimes they are like a compass, showing where north is but not how to get there or what will be there when we arrive. At other times, they are like a map that shows exactly how to get there.

The inner artist of our true Self uses two brushes: a conscious one in synchronicity, and an unconscious one in dreams. The synchronicities of our lives and the dream images that have most excited or stupefied us are the best—though often most ambiguous—clues to our self-actualization. When a dream confirms a movement in the psyche, that is itself synchronicity.

If we become too one-sided consciously, our psyche will shower us not only with dreams but also with coincidental events and relationships that commandeer us to visit the other side. For instance, if we are overly controlling, things will happen that topple our house of cards. To work with synchronicity is to go along with such a program and let its light through.

Thus, our psyche is the algebra expert with two favorite ways of reaching a pleasing equation. It can compensate for one-sidedness by dealing the opposite to us, or it can present a third solution to us as we are holding two alternatives and not acting on either. The unique shapes of the synchronicities that cluster around us tell us which program is in place.

Dreams work with synchronicity when they confirm or challenge steps and transitions that face us. They do this by foretelling the future, sending or receiving information before the linear mind can know it, and presenting the very images that help us find our path. In this sense, all images are assisting forces. In dreams, as in synchronicity, opposites unite and paradox reigns. This follows from the fact that the psyche is a balanced whole that transcends logical distinctions. Synchronicity and dreams balance the ego's exaggerations and its unlived, disowned characteristics. Dreams and synchronicity compensate for the biases of the ego and can rectify them too.

There is synchronicity also in a series of dreams. Reading through a journal in which we've recorded our dreams can make the apparently inchoate assemblage of recent dreams suddenly coherent. Specific themes or images appear more than once and point to a more orderly proceeding within and around us than we might ever have suspected. This is the inner shaping of individuation. Dreamwork—the techniques that follow—make the process conscious.

> Dreams prepare, announce or warn about situations long
> before they happen. This is not a miracle or precognition.
> Most crises have a long incubation in the unconscious.
> —CARL JUNG

REMEMBERING DREAMS
AND LEARNING FROM THEM

Interest and focus are the keys to a good memory. This applies to remembering dreams. The more you pay attention to the process of remembering, the more you remember. The more effort you put into remembering, the more you will remember. "Attention to the unconscious pays it a compliment that guarantees its cooperation," says Jung. Here are some specific suggestions:

- Keep a pad and pen or recorder by the bed, planning to use them upon awakening from each dream during the night. You will easily fall back to sleep. Upon awakening during the night, write or dictate only key phrases that summarize the dream. In the morning, they will trigger the rest of the dream, which can be recorded in your journal.

- Use autosuggestion throughout the day and while falling asleep: "I am remembering my dreams, waking up, and writing them down."
- Wake up naturally, without an alarm.
- Avoid sharp body movements as you awaken. These tend to jostle short-term memory.
- As you awaken, keep your eyes closed after a dream lest you be seduced and distracted by objects in the bedroom. With your eyes closed, review key elements in the dream and jot them down.
- The more you drop the need for an explanation, the more you access the dream world beyond the ordinary ego-mind.
- Review these dream categories to remember a dream:
    Characters: friends, family, famous, mythic, strangers
    Nature: tree, bird, stars, water, etc.
    Objects: clothes, weapons, tools, buildings, etc.
    Modifiers: small, big, ugly, etc.
    Emotions: joy, anger, fear, grief, compassion
    Sensations: warmth, cold, senses
    Setting: home, work, theater, church, indoor/outdoors, strange/familiar, etc.
    Conditions: weather, alone or with others, silence or sound
    Outcomes: fail, win, resolved/unresolved, happy/unhappy
    Interactions: fight, play, cooperate, compete, sexual behavior
- Use a sense exercise: picture a dream image in your mind, then move it, smell it, listen to its sounds, notice its surroundings, etc.

Once a dream is remembered, tell or write it, then retell it in the present tense. Notice what you may add or subtract in the second telling. Give the dream a title and a one-sentence summary. Make note of the context of the day. Notice where the dream fits in a series of dreams with similar themes. Notice colors, textures, smells. All dreams are in color, but color is forgotten first. It is useful to make note of colors first when you recall and write a dream. Treat each object as individual, not general (this lynx, not a lynx), and as alive since there is lively energy in every person, place, or thing in a dream.

Associate from each image by asking yourself, "What does this lead me to think of?" Identify with images and characters by playing each part. Each person and thing may be a part of yourself not yet integrated. Converse with images and characters in an inner dialogue. Finish imaginatively what is unfinished in the dream. Notice what was left out and bring it in. Answer unanswered questions. Experiment with different endings and notice the feelings that follow.

Pay special attention to setting, bodily and emotional reactions, and what may this dream be compensating for. Distinguish objective meanings—for example, family members or significant others appearing in picture-perfect form, which usually represent themselves—from subjective meanings—for example, dream figures, strangers, or " it looked like Ma but was not." These are often symbols of parts of ourselves that ask for attention or integration.

Ask yourself these questions about objects or themes in dreams: What part of me feels like that? What place feels like that place? What in my life makes me feel like that? What needs to be let go of or taken hold of? What part of me am I abandoning, fearing, rejecting? How is my life like this? See objects and events of the day as direct addresses to you, as assisting and afflicting forces.

Dreams are meant to be lived with as friends, not analyzed as patients. We gain more from a dream when we allow it to reveal itself to us than when we try to interpret it and pin it down to one meaning. No dream has a single meaning. The meaning of a dream may change with time. Let the dream unfold itself. I see my cat sitting on a chair. I can wonder when she will jump off. I can insist on answering this question and even become agitated by the suspense. Or I can simply keep observing her and sooner or later I will see her jump, and then I will know when she jumped. Practice being patient with a dream, allowing it to leap to you with meaning when it is ready.

The fact that an image in a dream is the same as or related to something that happened the day before does not mean that its significance is less potent. The dream-maker is a casting director using any people, things, and events to tell you your story. Dreams are not literal but metaphorical and symbolic. The symbolism is not diminished by the familiarity of the images any more than a film has less meaningfulness because it stars a familiar actor or uses props from another film. Look for symbols without forcing them from your images.

There is no morality in dreams. Stealing, for instance, may mean relocating energy to make it ready for a new use. Hermes and Prometheus stole to help mankind. They live as archetypes in us, as do all the heroes and villains we have met in fact and fiction. Notice how dreams show you your own projections through the strange characters you meet in dreams.

Interpretation is suspicious if it coincides with expectation since the unconscious is compensatory, not parallel, to our wishes or needs. Look for what is missing in your life more than for what you want fulfilled. In any case, interpretation is not the main point of dreamwork; engaging with the images to find their lively energy is. James Hillman writes of the main purpose in dreamwork: "The golden rule in tending any dream is keeping it alive. Dreamwork is conservation."

Never accept "I don't know!" Find the place in you where knowledge waits to be discovered. Make up something and see how it fits.

Dream images may metamorphose: "I saw a dog, but then he turned into a man." The first form is usually meant to lead to the more significant form. Follow the lead of the first version to the second and speak to it.

Animals in a dream are often guides to rich deposits in the unconscious mine. In your pondering on their appearance in your dream, follow them. Alice found a new world when she followed the white rabbit. Dorothy found her power to get home when she followed Toto, who had jumped from the dirigible.

Pay most attention to what engages, disgusts, or puzzles you.

If you are self-destructive in a dream, ask yourself what in your ego may be blocking development.

A sense of isolation in a dream may mean a unique development not yet seen by others. Recall that any higher consciousness is often a form of loneliness since those around you may not grasp what you have grasped.

The more active you are in a dream, the more involved you are in your conscious process, for example, "I planted flowers" versus "I saw flowers being planted." Notice the times in your journal you are writing in each mode.

It is a sign of progress when dreams no longer use symbols for feelings (for example, fire for anger) but feelings occur in the dream directly. Notice what you feel upon awakening. That feeling may be a signal of something ready to be expressed or at least acknowledged.

Be aware of the judgments you make about your dreams, such as, "I had a bad dream." There are no bad dreams. "Bad" shows what something unlived or unacknowledged looks like when it is repressed. You are finding out not how bad you are but how badly some part of you wants to be exposed and dealt with. Ask what that may be without fear of knowing.

Another judgment may be, I must be a terrible person and have such evil things in me to have such dreams!" All of us contain all the images of mankind. All of us have the collective human shadow inside. "Yet in thy dark streets shineth an everlasting light," says an old Christmas carol. There is a creative kernel in every dark image, a potential for light and goodness. It appears when we stop seeing ourselves as bad. Look for that valuable kernel.

Keep track of the dream themes or images that recur each time you begin a new enterprise. This may help you know more about an upcoming decision. For example, you notice that the image of a car that will not start has appeared in your dream journal before enterprises that have failed. Perhaps, that image is a caution about a choice that is coming up.

Use these same techniques in daily life, especially to ground yourself in situations that may seem strange or surreal!

Dreams are the native language of the unconscious.

—CARL JUNG

RECURRENT DREAMS

The Zeigarnik effect is a theory stating that an uncompleted task returns to memory and presses for completion whereas completed tasks remain quiet. This is how recurrent dreams can point to a continuing defect or excess that clamors for attention. They may also indicate a trauma not yet assimilated. The image is repeated in dreamland to help us absorb and integrate its far-flung shock. Recurrent dreams can also anticipate a development in the psyche. They are recurrent because something wants to come in: "Who knocks so loudly?" asks Friar Laurence in Shakespeare's *Romeo and Juliet*.

Common examples of recurrent dream themes are: fear of falling, a car will not start or stop, unpreparedness for an exam, rescuing of a child, being caught in a cataclysm, lateness, the inability to leave or get in, exclusion, nudity, animals. We may also meet recurrent dream places, a setting of the dream story that is known or unknown. This fits with the ancient belief that healing is often associated with specific places, for example, the Aesculapian temples, the Ganges, Machu Picchu, Lourdes.

Synchronicity and recurrent dreams are linked when they both seem to point to the same message. I may have a series of dreams in which I am losing my grip and then suffer a diminution of my powers in my conscious life. Dreams will often confirm or deny a choice that I have made and that has great consequences. Since the external and internal worlds are two sides of a single coin of consciousness, the world of action and the world of dreams actively unite.

ARCHETYPAL DREAMS

> Dreams point to a higher potential health, not simply past
> crises . . . giving clues to the archetypes of the psyche
> pressing for recognition.
>
> —JOSEPH CAMPBELL

Archetypes are recurrent typical themes of the human psyche that
appear as images or characters in stories and myths the world over.
The archetypes are fields of psychic energy within the Self. They pro-
pose a spiritual challenge to the ego to live out each energy or at least
relate to it in others. Archetypes include themes familiar in world religions: death-resurrection, transformation, epiphanies, ascension,
mystical marriage, judgment, punishment, etc. Archetypes are also
personified in stories as the hero, the shadow, the wise guide, the
trickster, the earth mother, the sky father, etc. Individuation happens
as we consciously integrate these unconscious drives—or instincts—
toward wholeness. Wholeness is in fact the integration of the archetypal potentials within us with those around us in our relationships
and experiences.

Most dreams come from our personal unconscious and tell us
about our ego work, that is, how to function in the world so that we
can fulfill ourselves and relate to others more effectively. These are
our psychological challenges. Some dreams, however, come from
our collective/cosmic unconscious and declare an archetypal task,
that is, a spiritual challenge. Archetypal images come to meet us in a
dream, carrying with them a grace or power to assist us in our conscious choices. This visit has a numinous quality. It is a spiritual vision
that beckons us onward and empowers us on our human trek toward
wholeness. Marie-Louise Von Franz puts it this way: "Whenever we
contact the deeper archetypal reality of the psyche, it permeates us
with a feeling of being in touch with the infinite."

Archetypal dreams grant us a glimpse of the invisible world, the
province of spirituality. Marvels of synchronicity are constant in the
psyche, a realm where nature's laws are not obeyed and ego limits are

continually transcended. Archetypal dreams are thus initiation rites into our spiritual work. Archetypal dreams occur in moments of crisis. They herald a transition, a time when a new strength is ready to surface or a new attitude is required to meet new challenges. The old or one-sided attitude no longer suffices. Oracular, ego-transcending wisdom of the archetypal Self emerges from deep in the psyche. The Delphic priestess has always been sitting here inside us, but we may never have traveled far enough within ourselves to consult her. Archetypal dreams are emitted from deep in nature, where she sits. They speak to us in her now-ready-to-be-audible voice.

How can we tell the difference between archetypal and personal dreams? Archetypal dreams unfold like an epic story, a journey, a struggle, a discovery. There is a sense of channeling, as if the dream came from a realm far beyond our routine world. We may feel a power that contains us; we do not contain it. Synchronicities will abound in waking life to match the motifs of such dreams. Strong feeling characterizes archetypal dreams and the memory of them. In fact, archetypal dreams are unforgettable—unlike many personal dreams. There is a strong sense of the numinous, the otherworldly in such dreams.

Archetypal dreams point directly to transformation. For example, I may dream that I am drowning in a vast and turbulent sea. Suddenly, a ghostly woman appears. She is hovering over the water beckoning to me to join her. I feel paralyzed and cannot manage that. A dolphin then arises beside and I look at him but do nothing. He then leaps up to her without me, splashing me with such force that I now seemed doomed for certain. I awake with fear and the sense that an opportunity to go beyond my habitual limits has been missed. I recognize the woman as a force of feminine power that challenges my reluctant consciousness and even offers me new powers and perspectives in the form of her dolphin friend. I keep pondering this dream throughout the day. What flying leaps am I afraid to take? What assisting force am I not hopping onto? What voice am I saying No to? What waters of rebirth am I still not allowing to drown my ego?

In times of strong feeling, the psyche will often produce an archetypal image in waking life. This is synchronicity. The psyche has a complete lexicon of images both from our life experience and from our ancestors', and it knows exactly which one fits an occasion. This is how our soul/synchronicity is helping us do our work. To work a conflict through in one's inner life leads to less need to obsess about it or dramatize it in one's daily life. This is because we focus on that center in ourselves where images are generated and where opposites are reconciled. As we relate to our own ego-transcending center, we make visible the wholeness that is already and always in us. Archetypal dreams connect our finite world of ego with the infinite world of wholeness.

Dreamwork is meant to be practiced with archetypal dreams, not just personal ones. Jung says: "Dreamwork releases an experience that grips or falls upon us as from above, an experience that has substance and body such as those things which occurred to the ancients. If I were to symbolize it, I would choose the Annunciation." The Annunciation to Mary by the angel Gabriel is an archetype of being open to receiving the tidings of destiny. The scene conveys in metaphor how our receptiveness to spiritual messages leads to the embodiment of transcendent purposes in us. Mary, symbolizing the willing ego, says yes unconditionally and becomes pregnant with Jesus, an archetype of wholeness. Synchronicities abound in this moment: the meeting of the angelic and the human, the male and the female, the immortal and the mortal, the transpersonal and the personal, the finite and the infinite, virginity and maternity, ego and Self, limitation and wholeness. Archetypal dreamwork facilitates such combinations.

The Annunciation means more than receiving tidings. In this event, we are touched by the zeal of the divine to enter our human condition and the joy of human nature to participate in it. "For every step the ego takes toward the Self, the Self takes one hundred toward the ego," wrote Jung, referring to the zeal of the Self for an embodiment in us.

DREAMWORK AND ACTIVE IMAGINATION

Synchronicity requires consciousness. In dreamwork we activate our conscious imagination to amplify the unconscious messages of dreams. Dreams want to find expression or completion in our waking world. Active imagination facilitates this since it activates the transcendent function of the psyche. Dreamwork is our synchronizing of unconscious message and conscious work. It is a way of expanding upon the themes and images in our dreams by dialoguing with them. This process becomes synchronicity as it honors the transcendent function of the psyche to unite and synthesize conscious and unconscious realms within us. The psyche channels images from the soul treasury within/beyond us. The psyche presents in dreams and in active imagination precisely the image that is required here and now for our rise in consciousness. This is the essence of the synchronicity of dreams, letting the light through so we can see in the dark.

"Imagination acts by impressing the stamp of humanity on inanimate or merely natural objects," says the poet Samuel Taylor Coleridge. Dreamwork is active imagination, engaging in a dialogue with an image or a figure from a dream. I let this image take me where *it* wants to go, no matter how outrageous the trip. The hero goes with the flow of events with a sense of wonder. The end of wonder is the end of staying on the journey. A fully developed experience or change is usually not possible in a dream state. A conscious elaboration is required: dreamwork, active imagination in the day about the night's dream.

Active imagination (described below) is like alchemy, in that attention is paid even to the lowliest elements, and their transformation follows. Active imagination makes an accommodation with our predicament, thereby negotiating a path through it. Active imagination is not simply a technique to observe the unconscious. In it the ego asserts itself and helps our unconscious see how its demands can or cannot match the conditions of reality. Dialogue helps us relate to the figures in our unconscious rather than be possessed by them, stand in awe of them, or be frightened by them. Images are immensely responsive to the compliment paid to them by our contemplation. They are given a voice by such attentiveness. This is how the active imagination expands and completes an image.

"Make the night joint laborer with the day," says Hamlet. Dreams initiate and present our work to us. Dreamwork is our way of picking it up from there. Dante recognized this during his three nights and three days in Purgatory. Each night he had a dream that he took time to contemplate during the following day. His dreams while unconscious were all part of the work of purification he was experiencing consciously. We are being freed and freeing ourselves night and day from our limited ego to expand into the wholeness we already are in the depths of ourselves. Active imagination is the daylight contribution we make to match the psyche's nightly contribution in dreams. There is optimistic synchronicity in that joint venture.

The Care and Tending of Dreams

Consider your dream from each of the following three perspectives:

> Intrapersonally: see all the figures of your dream as parts of your inner world.
> Interpersonally: your dream shows you your way of relating to others.
> Transpersonally: your dream tells you about your spiritual life and destiny.

Amplify your dream by using the various forms of active imagination described below.

Empty your mind of left-brain or distracting thoughts: "I let go of ordinary thinking and analyzing. I am open to the voice that wants to come through to me." "Empty" also means empty of fear and attachment, that is, empty of ego.

Look at the image in your dream that most engages you, noticing the "felt sense" of it: As I hold this image, what do I feel, and where do I feel it in my body? Which of the seven chakras, or physical-spiritual energy centers within the body, is this image most comfortable in: survival (base of spine), sex (genitals), power (solar plexus), heartfulness (heart), release of free speech (throat), wisdom, or spiritual power (above the crown of the head)?

Using your dream journal, dialogue with (and become) the image. Add the phrase: "This is part of myself" to an image, or "This is my life (or body)" to a scene. Make associations until you reach an "Aha!"—a satisfying sign of finding your personal meaning in a dream.

Choose nine words from all you have written to create a poem.

Ask for a gift or message with thanks for what may come.

Form an affirmation or aspiration that declares the message or central point of your dream and use it throughout the day.

Perform a ritual that enacts the message, including thanks for all it has meant to you.

8

Synchronicity and Our Spirituality

The more we become conscious of ourselves through self-knowledge,
and act accordingly, the more the layer of the personal unconscious
will be diminished. In this way, there arises a consciousness no longer
imprisoned in petty personal interests. This widened consciousness ...
is a function of our relationship to the world ... bringing us
into an absolute binding and indissoluble communion with the
universe. ... There is no individuation on Everest.
—CARL JUNG

Spiritual work does not begin with action but with centered attentiveness to the messages of our inner Self in synchronicity, dreams,
and intuitions. Now we understand that our inner Self refers to an
unconscious depth in ourselves that we share with all humanity and
that funds our lives with spiritual gifts when we are open to it. In
such a spiritual world, we keep finding exactly the discarded pieces
of ourselves that clamor for reattachment to our psyche. This is how
synchronous meetings and messages impel us to wholeness.

Spirituality is the intersection of three paths: letting go of ego, an
unconditional Yes to the conditions of human existence, and universal

compassion. Synchronicity meets us on all three of these paths. These paths open by work on ourselves—steps we take—and by grace from assisting forces around us—shifts that happen. There is synchronicity built into this combination of effort and grace. Effortful steps open us to effortless shifts. We work diligently on ourselves and transformation happens from and within that momentum.

Work on ourselves means traveling the three paths of spirituality in psychologically healthy human living. Here is an overview of this work:

Letting go of ego means freeing ourselves from self-centered entitlements and from the need to be in control. Such letting go is a challenge to the part of us that insists on being first and right. It is a nonviolent style that drops competitiveness and self-seeking in favor of humility and equality. Synchronously, just the right people and events will come our way so that this can happen. We will definitely get our comeuppance and be liberated from our ego inflations as we meet up with our fellow pilgrims. They will also help us transform our neurotic ego into a healthy ego.

We say Yes unconditionally to the conditions and predicaments of our existence: things change and end, suffering is part of growth, things are not always predictable or fair, etc. We assent to these givens of life because we trust them as necessary ingredients for us to grow and deepen. Spiritual progress does not mean that we are always serene or happy but that we have a formula to accommodate any state of mind: an unconditional Yes to what is unfolding. This Yes is how we become synchronicity. We then identify our personal story with a larger picture. When we reconcile ourselves to the conditions of our existence, when we reconcile the opposing forces in our psyche, and when we reconcile ourselves to others, too, many stunning marvels begin to happen.

Compassion means acting with love and a caring heart toward those who suffer. A personal awakening brings with it an inner zeal for others to be awakened too. This emerges from a sense of solidarity with all beings and with all of nature—the very point of synchronicity. *Tikkun olam* is a Hebrew phrase meaning "repair of the world." Such engaged concern is the proof positive of an authentic spirituality for it does not end in "feel good" but in "do good." It is not simply about consolation for our minds but consecration of our hearts to this needy world.

Every pain and grief I meet is an address to me to enter the desperation of those who may not be able to find the Taoist "mysterious pass through the apparently impenetrable mountains." The desperate dislocation that occurs corresponds to the dismemberment of the hero/redeemer—a metaphor of the divesting of ego—for the sake of suffering humanity. Our letting go of ego is meant to be the threshold to compassion.

Compassion is not an ideal but a phenomenon of higher consciousness, the new consolidation of ego-I with Self-world. Its purpose is to reorganize the ego around an all-embracing love. Universal love is how the ego becomes spiritually coherent—as it becomes psychologically coherent by being personally loved and loving. Compassion does not mean noticing pain or even understanding it empathically. Empathy is the mirroring of pain in others. Compassion *activates* our empathy; it does something about it. Yet true compassion is indeliberate and automatic too. It is like the moon, which makes no specific decision to reflect itself in the pond. It simply lets it happen without planning or parceling.

The Dalai Lamas are believed to be incarnations of Avalokitesvara, the Buddha of compassion. He is depicted with many heads to see the suffering of mankind from every direction. He has a thousand arms to reach out everywhere and an eye in the palm of each hand since compassion is not blind. This is a metaphor of the spontaneous urge toward compassion flowing from the wisdom of letting go of the sense of separate, rather than interdependent, existence. Once we are free of the illusion of separateness, we feel responsible for one another.

We notice in the *Heart Sutra* that Avalokitesvara, the bodhisattva of compassion, presents the doctrine of nonduality and of the emptiness of ego, not Sariputra, the bodhisattva of intellectual knowledge. The wisdom of the awakened heart (*bodhicitta*) motivates the enlightened person to give up liberation for himself alone in favor of the liberation of others. Tara, the Mother of all Buddhas and the female aspect of compassion, was formed from a teardrop of Avalokitesvara. She vowed to help him free all of us from the fetters of fear and grasping. Buddha himself is said to be born from compassion. He also lives to show compassion and to show it reliably and universally. This is why the practitioner says, "I take refuge in the Buddha."

Compassion is a state of mind flowing from the realization of emptiness, that is, no inherent, self-sustaining existence in any thing or person. We are all interdependent both among ourselves and between us and all of nature. Awareness of this profound, primal, and indestructible unity leads us to mutual reverence and caring love. This is one way the wisdom of nonduality connects us to compassion.

Once we perceive the ultimate oneness of all beings, a solidarity results between us and them. This is our capacity to love without fear. This is the fearlessness that reckons every event and encounter in life as happening at just the right time and in just the right way for us to learn what we need to know. In such a synchronous world, nothing can go wrong, at least not for long. That trust becomes the basis of fearlessness. How does this fearlessness happen? A compassionate act shatters the walls that divide us and reveals the touching similarities that make us no longer so different from one another. The unconditional love, immortal wisdom, and healing power of the Self are then seen not as virtues we achieve but as natural consequences of spiritual liberation. Now personal liberation is equated with liberation of all beings since there is no separate I on whom to dote.

The bodhisattva path is the altruistic mind of enlightenment, now operating automatically and spontaneously in daily actions. One's personal enlightenment is now secondary, a means to the goal of bringing others to enlightenment, not vice versa. A bodhisattva sees others' suffering and pledges herself to their release from it in the same instant. She expends as much effort as if she could single-handedly do it. Thereafter, even receiving the appreciation of others is done for their sake.

Buddha's message is about the utterly disappointing emptiness of the ego to satisfy us. In the tantric practice of Buddhism, this refuge in ego is not a sign of failure. It is how we finally notice what our mind is and what it can and cannot offer us. This recognition is the path to practices that will help us toward egolessness. Compassion toward others is one of those practices.

"Someday, I suppose it will become evident that the laws in the Torah are meant to lead to a universal love of humanity," said the first-century Jewish historian Josephus, who knew that spiritual and religious practice has one and only one purpose: to increase our love. In fact, giving is the best way to free ourselves from the fears and attachments that make us so unhappy. This is because love is the only life purpose that can be worthy of beings like us. How is it expressed? It is shown in engaged and tangible ways: feeding the hungry, clothing the naked, sheltering the homeless, responding to human need. It is also a feeling response to human needs: compassion to the afflicted, comfort to the grieving, forgiveness of injury, redressing injustice, etc. This fits with the bodhisattva's "four means to help others": to give what is needed, to speak gently, to console and guide, and to be an example of active love.

Martin Luther King Jr. gave a sermon on the disciples' asking of Jesus if they could sit on his right and left side in the new kingdom. They construed the kingdom to be about ego that is, making sure they would get what they were entitled to. King pointed out that those special places are reserved for the people who feed the hungry, clothe the naked, etc. This is a perfect summary of spirituality: letting go of ego and showing love concretely.

Toward the end of his sermon, Martin Luther King said, "Every once in a while I think of my death and I wonder how I will be remembered. I hope my eulogist won't mention my Nobel Peace Prize, my education, my other awards. . . . I want to be remembered as one who tried to love somebody. Let him say that Martin Luther King tried to feed the hungry, to clothe the naked, to visit the imprisoned, to help the blind see and the deaf hear. . . . I have nothing to leave you, no riches, no luxury. All I leave behind is a committed life. Jesus, I don't want to be on your right or left side because of fame but because of love."

Spirituality is just such an engaged and committed life. It grants us hope, the conviction that behind the appearance of this latest triumph of evil is the ultimate and lasting victory of goodness. Our hope persists not because injustices have finally ended but because they are not final. They are not final because *we* are not returning evil for evil and thus perpetuating it. They are not final because we are still here transmitting restorative love and reconciliation. A seventeenth-century Japanese poem says, "If you keep one green bough in your heart, someday a singing bird will visit you." *What makes this believable is the good thing I did today for someone in need.*

In English, the word *nemesis* means a source of harm or ruin, one's downfall. In ancient Greece, Nemesis was revered as the goddess/personification of retributive justice. Her second name is Adrasteia, which means "inescapable." In Homer, her name means "due enactment." When Tyche, goddess of luck and windfalls, bestowed fortune on someone, Nemesis, goddess of downfalls, stepped in to humble him if he arrogantly boasted, did not use part of his wealth to alleviate the poverty of others, or refused to sacrifice to the gods in thanksgiving, that is, denied the element of grace in his good fortune. This is a colorful way of declaring that the touch of grace was historically associated with letting go of ego, acknowledging grace, and having the instinct for generosity and compassion.

Notice also how the three criteria that Nemesis looks for are precisely the foundation principles of spirituality: transcendence of ego, appreciation of grace, and compassion for others. All through the ages, in every spiritual tradition, we see this same expansive threefold sense of human potential and destiny. Buddhists affirm that when bodhisattvas and saints catch a glimpse of us loving in this way—no matter how secretly we do it—they hasten to our side to assist and encourage us. The guardian angel metaphor points to the assisting force of grace. Love attracts grace; ego repels it.

To love is to enter the synchronicity of grace. In love, the most striking of all coincidences occurs: two hearts or all hearts match in their encounter and enfolding of each other. Each grants the very tenderness the other wanted all his life to find or waited all his life to find again.

Love is the only bridge that hearts can toss across the yawning void of emptiness that the mind will make.

Love is the fire that can melt the ego in an instant.

Love forgives every offense with exactly the brand of healing that makes new offenses unlikely.

Love reaches beyond "I and Thou" to all living beings in far-flung compassion and unconditional caring.

Love lets go, never losing what it has once held.

Love lives on, never ending what it has begun.

Love remains steadfast, never abandoning what it has committed itself to.

Love is the rendezvous of closing and opening, of kneading and rising, of hungering and banqueting, of halting and dancing, of living and dying.

In love there is neither yours nor mine but only everyone's Yes to the grace of opening.

> I have opened a door for you that no one can close.
>
> —REVELATION 3:8

MAKING LOVE CONCRETE

1. Prior to an activity or project in daily life, form an altruistic intention to bring enlightenment to others through what you are about to do. This form of the practice of loving-kindness locates our activities in the context of generous compassion. Upon completion of the activity, dedicate its value to the welfare of people and nature and to the increase of love in the world.

2. Aspirations can also evoke love. Repeat them until your love becomes spontaneous, universal, and continuous.

May I become ever more engaged in loving service.

May the whole purpose of my life be to put everything I
do into the channel of universal love.

May I work for the harmony and reconciliation of all
beings.

May I consecrate myself to nonviolence in the face of
every conflict.

May I be stirred by the pain I see in the world and may I
make a loving response to it.

Practice this love with specific individuals as well as to the
world at large. Extend love especially to people with whom
you have a karmic connection since they are the ones most in
need of your love.

3. Do little favors each day for friends and then for strangers
too, without calling attention to what you have done for
them. Buddha himself said, "When your path is secret even
from gods, angels, or human beings, you are truly priestly." If
you begin to feel a sense of obligation or compulsion in this
practice, discontinue it. Begin again when you can do it with
choice and generosity. Most of us have habituated ourselves
to misleading information about our capacity for love. It is
infinitely vaster than we ever dared imagine. Little acts of
love grant the best entry into the overstuffed treasury.

4. One effective way to bring meditation into action is to carry
out this resolve: "For every grace I ask, I ask the same for
others. For every grace I receive, I give something of myself
to others as a form of thanks." This is an example of loving-
kindness in our spiritual life. A transformation has happened
when I have gone beyond the goal of handling things, that is,
helping myself. I am now working for the higher stakes of
healing the world. An equation has occurred between my
work on myself and my commitment to my fellow humans.

5. Try any one of these once each day in any simple way that
may work: Demonstrate your love for specific people in
some concrete way. Find a community program that helps

you feed the hungry, clothe the naked, shelter the homeless, or care for those in physical need. Offer a feeling response to the emotional needs of people in your life: compassion for the afflicted, comfort for the grieving, forgiveness of injury.

6. The Sermon on the Mount (in Matthew, chapters 5–7), based on rabbinical teachings, has become the Christian recipe for the dismantling of the arrogant, self-centered ego. It proposes nonviolent techniques as ways of showing love. Read it and imagine what your life would be like if you closely followed it. Take one example of a current conflict with someone and apply Jesus's recommendations. Notice how you feel about yourself. What happens to you when you no longer care about winning, being right, or retaliating? How have you thereby found a sector of your inner Self that was perhaps unexplored before? *Is the Sermon on the Mount perhaps a portrait of us at our best—what we would look like if we were not afraid of love?*

7. The Greek word for sin is *hamartia* which literally means "missing the target." Our collective human target is love, wisdom, and healing. We each show these in our own ways. Sin is a deliberate choice not to employ those three powers. It is any act that overrides our spiritual instinct for wholeness and thus makes us miss the target of collective and individual destiny. Write an inventory of how have you hurt, betrayed, or abandoned yourself or others in choices you have made or in habits you have maintained. Look for compassion for yourself, not blame. Look for compassion for others, not disregard. Make amends to yourself and others by admitting your wrongs, asking pardon, making specific amends for the losses and/or pain you have caused, and resolving to change your life so that you do not continue in the old way. The sight of you showing contrition, amendment, and resolution may disarm the other and free him/her to forgive you, that is, let go of blaming or hating you.

Here is a model that may help in designing your inventory:

How have I been an afflicting force in the lives of others? I
may have been offensive in words said or neglected to
be said, or in actions, both done and left undone.
Some of these transgressions are known only to me
and some are felt by and known to others.

What deliberate choices have I made that have been abusive, led to hurt, or caused a loss?

What agreements have I broken?

How have I acted (or failed to act) *because* of fear and
thereby lost access to my courage?

How have I acted with an arrogant or entitled ego?

Apply this same model to yourself. How have you hurt
yourself or let others hurt you?

What is the best chance love can have to work in your
life from now on?

Use each of the points in the above model now in reverse: How
have I been an assisting force in others' lives?

How to Stay and See

Stand stable here
And silent be . . .
Here at the small field's ending, pause . . .
—W. H. Auden, from *"On This Island"*

In this section, we pull together some of the more salient ideas of
the book and show how they can work for us.

We are aware of our psychological needs: attention, acceptance,
affection, appreciation, and allowing. Some of our spiritual needs
have become evident in the course of these pages: opening to intuitions and synchronicities that point to or confirm a path for us, initiatory experiences that may lead to a letting go of ego, finding
wisdom, and showing compassion.

As the fulfillment of psychological needs results in a coherent sense of identity, the fulfillment of spiritual needs results in a grateful sense of wholeness. Identity is something we work for; wholeness is who and what we always and already are. Spiritual needs lead to a realization and manifestation of wholeness not to the creation of it. Psychological work takes effort and willpower. Spiritual practice takes responsiveness to grace (forces that assist us in transcending our limited will and intellectual powers) and willingness to pronounce the unconditional Yes to that which is.

Psychological work begins with acknowledging the issue that faces us. We then can address, process, and resolve it. What is the spiritual way of handling what comes up in our lives? It may begin with looking for ground in the artistic sense of that word. In the *Mona Lisa,* the woman is figure and the background (landscape with the river, etc.) is ground. As long as I focus on the figure, I miss the ground. An issue or conflict that faces me in life is the figure. What is the ground? It must be something unnoticed, perhaps invisible.

In fact, behind all appearances is a reality that is invisible to the eye. Wordsworth refers to the sudden, synchronous "flash of the mystery of the invisible world." The whole of a reality is figure *and* ground. So wholeness is what we miss when we see in our habitually narrow ways. We see even less when we are obsessed by any one person or thing. This is the real danger in fear and grasping.

To stay is to stay with what is, responsive to its rhythms rather than imposing our own. To stay in this way means staying without controlling, desiring, fearing, expecting, or judging. *To see* is to release ourselves from obsession with our predicament, to enter the space behind the appearances, the ground behind the figure. To stay and see is the synchronicity of mindfulness because we are aligned to reality without the usual screens of ego in the way.

I do not see the whole picture when I focus on one thing, that is, when I am caught up in a compelling drama or a rigid interpretation of it. How can I contact the ground, the greater perspective? I need more than focused attention if I am to see fully. A diffuse attention is necessary, the attentiveness and presence that happen in mindfulness.

The Sanskrit word for mindfulness actually comes from two words meaning "attend" and "stay." Simply to sit in the space around our reality is mindfulness in it. This is meditation on our present moment rather than control of it.

A spiritual approach to our conflicts begins with a *breather* for dropping out of the drama, a recess from the struggle, a release from its grip. Instead of continually focusing on the conflict, we take a break. We let our drama fade from view for the moment and concentrate instead on the space around it. This is the pause we have been referring to throughout this book. It is the rest in music, unheard but essential for its pleasing flow.

As long as I am caught up in dramatic storylines of fear or desire, I fail to hear the rich spiritual rhythms in my life. Mindfulness opens me to a wider context in my story beyond the content of it. The content is psychological (figure); the context is spiritual (ground). My work will always be in both areas. Then I do not "miss the many-splendored thing," as the poet Francis Thompson says.

Here are some further examples of the two perspectives.

Figure	*Ground*
Conscious	Unconscious
Ego	Self
Persona	Shadow
False self	True Self
Thought	Imagination
Logic	Intuition
Words	Silence
Cause/effect	Synchronicity
Fear	Excitement
Desire	Plenitude
Transitions	Heroic journey
Psychological work	Spiritual practices
Holding on	Letting go
"I"	Universe

Every psychological crisis is a loss of something we were holding onto. Around and within this loss is its ground, its space. This space is the power to let go. In fact, what can be lost needed to be let go of anyway. What is real cannot be lost at all: unconditional love, wisdom, the power to do our work on ourselves and to bring healing into the world. Only the ego's goods can be lost, not the powers of the Self. Since spiritual practice is required for the letting go of ego grasping, spirituality is the ground of our psychological work. This is how we can see that psychology and spirituality are integrated. It also explains why spirituality is not disembodied from our story but the fuller dimension of it.

Space, or ground, is what makes something more than what it appears to be, more than I fear it is limited to be. I am more than meets the eye and so is everything. I and everything are therefore whole: figure and ground, visible and invisible, psychological and spiritual. This is another way of accounting for the unity of all beings, all equally arising from the deathless, pure, open ground of existence, the void over which the Spirit brooded on the day of creation.

This space is also referred to in Zen as *shunyata*. It may be feared by the frantic ego as a sterile void or a black hole. Actually, it is a fecund void because it offers us the wider and widening dimensions of any reality. Such a spacious void is the ground that underlies wholeness, a limitless openness. It grants us, finally, what nothing else can, room to move. Is this what we ultimately fear, the room to move on? Is this why we keep heaven closed till after death? "I saw Heaven open," says Revelation 19:11. *Dare we glimpse it now?* That heaven is the space in our hearts that lets love through "and makes one little room an everywhere," as John Donne says.

Space happens between two planes. A pause occurs between two actions. Celtic spirituality has a fascination with the sacred realm of the *between*: the place or moment when the veils between the physical and spiritual worlds are so thin that we easily cross over. The space we have been contemplating is the between. It is the threshold as a beach is a threshold between the land and the ocean or adolescence is a threshold between childhood and adulthood. This mysterious

between-world has appeared in every chapter of this book: soul is between ego and Self; synchronicity happens between cause and
chance; mirroring happens between I and Thou; dreamwork occurs
between unconscious and conscious; poetry arises between prose
words and wordless communication; destiny opens between effort
and grace; love thrives between letting go and going on. This same
between is in the transcendent function of the psyche that produces
the healing third when we hold two opposites. By synchronicity,
every moment stands on the threshold between time and eternity—
and lets us stand there too. In fact, since any moment offers the possibility of awakening, every moment is synchronicity.

> It is by coincidence that I have discovered the enlightenment
> spirit inside me.
>
> —SHANTIDEVA

WORKING IN SPACE

1. King Bimbisara gave the Buddha a bamboo grove near Raja-
   griha to be used as a retreat. Picture it as you imagine it to be
   and go there now in your heart. The human heart is, after all,
   the bamboo grove, the spacious retreat in which you can
   pause and be silent and unseen for awhile and from which
   you emerge to be articulate and eminently visible, when the
   time for that comes.
2. How do we work in the ground-space of our story? The first
   and most powerful way is mindfulness, a technique we can
   use daily. Here is another exercise:

Write a sentence (using one of the models below) about your
present personal crisis or issue. Begin with the words *either . . . or,
if . . . then,* or *because . . . I.* Here are examples of completed sentences: Either I stay in control, or everything will fall apart. Either I
stay with you unhappily, or I leave you unwillingly. If they find out,

then I lose my job (or reputation, etc.). Because you left me, I intend to punish you.

| Either I stay in control | , | or everything will fall apart. |

Draw a box around each of the two clauses with the comma unboxed in the center. Study your sentence with its boxes, the space between them and around them. The boxes are the figure and the space is the ground. See if your eye can reverse figure and ground for a few seconds so that the space becomes something. Look steadily at the comma. A comma in speech represents a pause. A pause is to the ear what space is to the eye. This comma has created a space. "Enter here" (literally) and pause now. Breathe evenly as you do this, paying attention to each in-breath and each out-breath and the little space between each breath.

Allow yourself to be with your statement while keeping the pause button pressed on all judgments, fears, desires, attachments to outcomes, etc. Experience your statement with clarity and pure awareness, with no layers of drama around it, only space around it. Simply stay in the space and attend to breathing there. This part may take the rest of the day—or of your life—and what better way could there be of spending it?

Notice the content of the sentence. Do you see a sense of necessity in it? Does the second part seem forced to follow from the first? This is dualism. It makes the sentence a "sentence" from a judge. Who is that judge? Do not attempt to integrate or combine the clauses of your statement. Instead, find an alternative that does not give in to either side of the dilemma. Notice that this cannot be done. You are stumped, the left brain's response to spiritual space.

Being stumped makes us feel powerless, so we fear space. We are fearing the gap that has opened in our heretofore reliable logical categories. We are fearing the space that undermines logic and underlies every reality—Rumi's "the field beyond right and wrong," Revelation's "heaven open," the Taoist "mysterious pass." As we continue simply to stay attentively, it will all yield and shift. The gap will become an opening. This is the *pause* that restores. Make no attempt to figure anything out. Simply breathe, letting go of the need to know anything, and paying attention to the space.

Here is what happened to the original sentences after this process:

"Either I stay in control . . . " became: "I let the chips fall where they may." I am not caught in having to control or in being the victim of chaos. I dropped into the space, fell into the gap, and there I found a way to live that releases me from the dilemma, is still responsible, and is much more realistic. (When I did this exercise myself, I laughed out loud when the "chips" sentence came to me. Humor is the ground of all our predicaments, comedy the ground of tragedy.)

"Either I stay with you unhappily . . . " becomes "We work together on changing things." "If they find out . . . " becomes "I will be the one to tell and will tell it proudly or with willingness to make amends and be done with it." This is how I am released from shame, the opposite of being mirrored. Now I can mirror myself. "Because you left me . . . " becomes "I let go of the need to punish you. I grieve your going and get on with my life." I am free of vengeance and open to compassion.

The new statements were there all along within the originals, in the space, the comma-pause. Each of them confers a power. Each new version is what your situation looked like before your ego got hold of it. The good witch said to Dorothy, "You've had the power all along! Just click your heels." Her power was the ground under her; the ground of power was under her illusory figural belief that she was powerless.

What actually happened in the movement from the figure to the ground of our personal story? We stripped our ego of its layers of judgments, fears, desires, and attachments and entered the mindful state in which the ego's knowledge is unnecessary or irrelevant. We did not know how to fix things, so we chose to know even less! There is a poem by Saint John of the Cross that begins with that same paradox: "I entered I knew not where and there I stood not knowing: nothing left to know. . . . " We did what Rembrandt did one day in his father's windmill: see a space in reflected light but see it as a form. This is like the Buddhist realization that "form is emptiness and emptiness form." Once this has happened to us even once, there is no going back to imprisonment in our dramas and to our habitual reactions to them. There is space and spacious perspective.

To contact this soul space, not filled in by drama, means attending to the headline and not the editorial. When we drop attachment to outcome, a gap opens in the ego's cycle of fear and craving. Surrender results. "I observe my life as a silent and fair witness who feels all feelings deeply but is not overwhelmed by any one of them." Usually, the story is the figure; the silence is the ground. In mindfulness, these are reversed. Our silent soul becomes the focus, the duck blind out of which we see the world flying by, but with no intent to catch it, only satisfaction in seeing it at last with equanimity and amusement.

We will still have a story, but not one we have to tell. We will still have fears, but not ones that stop us. We will still have desires, but not ones that blind us. We will, in fact, have "ever more perfect eyes in a world in which there is always more to see," as Teilhard de Chardin says. Our spiritual capacity may never be large enough to accommodate all the light that shines on us—no more than our capacity to exult in the days of our children's infancy ever lasted long enough to contain all the joy they were beaming upon us.

We are learning to hold the tension of opposites. We feel a sense of equanimity as we simply pause long enough to hold them as "both . . . and" rather than "either . . . or." Here is a mythic example: A decorated vase found in ancient Sicily is mentioned in Robert Graves's book *Greek Myths*. The picture on the vase shows the hero Theseus, robed as an annual king, with his arms outstretched. Into his left hand, Pasiphae, wife of the dark minotaur, is placing an apple. Into his right hand, her daughter Ariadne, who guided him out of the dangerous labyrinth into the light, is placing the gift of an egg. An annual king is a figure from antiquity who ruled for four seasons only. Apples appear in the autumn and hence were associated with upcoming endings and death, as we notice later in our Judeo-Christian story of Adam and Eve. The outgoing king was given an apple to signify the end of his rule. The new king received an egg, symbol of new life. The fact that Theseus receives both at once is a striking way of saying that we are always in the midst of endings and beginnings and that we are heroic enough to *handle* that fact.

Like the mythic king, we can pronounce a double Yes to what begins and what has to end. When faced with dilemmas, contradictions, and confusion, we can use the simple practice of holding out our hands and imagining we are holding both realities that face us. We hold the apple and the egg each day in some way. We are always letting go of something or someone and taking hold of something or someone else. The challenge is to say Yes unconditionally to both. This is the combination of opposites that makes equanimity possible.

For example, we want to be more assertive and yet we want to have humility too. We picture these possibilities in the palm of each hand, cupped, palms up, noticing that they weigh the same—nothing at all. We can easily carry both. We affirm that, and gradually we notice our behavior follows suit. When disparate energies are held in this inclusive way, they generate an acceptance and a discerning wisdom.

This acceptant Yes to a "both . . . and" is another example of the style of not doing, or *wu wei* in Taoism. It implies that all that is happening is happening just as it needs to. There is no need to take control of others or manipulate events. *Wu wei* thus works as an affirmation of inevitable fulfillment. I simply let be, say Yes to what is, and allow what wants to happen. Those are the behaviors of someone who is content with reality and fulfilled by it.

READY FOR BIRTH

> Man does not change at death into his immortal part, but is mortal and immortal even in life, being both ego and Self.
> —CARL JUNG

Synchronicity is the keystone of the arch of psychological and spiritual integration. It is up to us to see it and be it. We are more apt to see synchronicity when we go beyond the limits of our linear mind and our clinging ego. We are synchronicity when we say Yes to the world that opens beyond ego. Grace enlivens and enriches our efforts to dismantle our narcissistic ego's fear and grasping so that we can say Yes unconditionally to the conditions of human existence, show universal love to human beings anywhere, and live in respectful harmony with nature everywhere. We human beings have a knack for reaching beyond our given limits. Our capacity for transcendence makes it possible for us to become open to grace. That is a short step to becoming aware of a Higher Power than our own ego. Synchronicity manifests this Power like a missionary proclaiming divine life to an ignorant but longing world.

"Initiation is a death to something which is ready to be surpassed. . . . Initiation is passing by way of symbolic death and resurrection from ignorance and immaturity to the spiritual age of an adult," wrote Mircea Eliade. Spiritual initiation adopts the same symbolism, as is seen in madness and chaos, that is, a dissolution of order. This is a metaphor for the dissolution of the profane ego, the ego without a Self. The eschatological symbol of this is the "end of the world." The afterlife, in this context, may mean that there is a continuity in Self-consciousness in all humanity. No such promise is made to the grasping ego.

Synchronicity comes into play when a new world/personality is ready for birth precisely as an initiatory death is undergone. The painful initiatory rites are stages of mystical death and rebirth and endow the psychic traveler with a new sensitivity to others. This sensitivity also means an ability to integrate and transform pain in oneself. Through this sensitivity, the spiritual synchronously manifests. Then we are, as Mircea Eliade writes, "born into an existence which, while it is lived to all appearances in this world of ours, is framed in other existential dimensions."

Thus there is something about our life story that does not depend upon our ego efforts. Something seems to beckon to us beyond what our minds produce or even desire. The paradox of the hero's journey is the ultimate synchronicity; it is found when it is no longer sought.

The confident samurai is no longer compelled to fight; he is happy to stand his ground as an amused witness of how reality will play itself out: "When I stop controlling and seeking, I find the infinite possibilities in the here and now. I land on reality that is immensely open. I move through it to what comes next. Here and now is the only reality available without seeking. Seeking is what diverts me from it. Desire blinds me to the joyous lark called Now singing to me Here. When desire for otherwise disappears, so does division." Synchronicity is connection and is thus a spiritual symbol of this freedom from separateness.

A symbol in Hinduism is the gander, who represents liberation and spirituality. He swims in and skims over the water but is not bound to it like a fish. He flies between earth and heaven and so joins them together. This is a metaphor for our ability to be set free from our bondage to the events of daily life. "Gander" in Sanskrit is *hamsa*. *Ham* means "I" and *sa* means "this"; hence "I am this." *Hamsa* is also yogic sound—*ham* on the exhale, *sa* on the inhale. Thus the inner gander sings his name in every breath we take: "I am not to be confused with the mortal person who has my name and who accepts as real the separateness of all beings, the division of opposites, and the linear view of time. That individual is under the spell of endless projections and mental habits. I am breath, space, the all that is now only this."

> I bring forth the universe from my essence and I abide in the cycle of time that dissolves it.
> —The *Myth of Markandeya*, FROM THE MARIYA PURANA

DECLARING AND DEDICATING

Ask yourself how your finding and reading of this book was an example of synchronicity. Write about it in your journal and tell one—or more—persons about it, verbally and in letters.

Look at the sections of this book that you have made note of or underlined. Read them onto a tape and listen to the tape once each

day for as many days as you may choose. Do the same with the quo-
tations that are scattered throughout the text.

Dedicate the work you have done in this book to the welfare of
the world, offering all your more lively love, your new knowledge,
and your healing powers to the treasury of wisdom from which all
we wanderers can draw. We are always reinvesting our graces and
progress in the vast treasury of human evolution: "When I achieve, I
share." Decide and declare that whenever you achieve an advance in
love or wisdom, you extend it to all your fellow humans, that they
might progress in the same ways. "Whenever and in whatever I expand, I extend."

When you feel truly happy, remember to say, "May all beings feel
this happiness with me." This practice of loving-kindness engenders
a view of happiness as a gift you have received in order to give it
away. Happiness is then not a personal possession but a bond with all
mankind. When you are sad or discouraged, remember that many
other people the world over are feeling what you are feeling at the
same time. Join with them: "May all those feeling what I am feeling
find a way through it. May they be helped by my work on myself.
May I be helped by theirs."

Here are more declarations that may fit:

I am thankful for the work I have accomplished and the graces I
have received in the reading and working of this book.

I acknowledge and appreciate the synchronicities in my daily life.

I acknowledge a meaning in every chaos.

I acknowledge a world beyond my senses, a truth beyond my intellect, a wisdom beyond logic, a power beyond my limits, a serene
design that abides despite any distressing display.

I am thankful for the graces that take me beyond my limits.

I seek community with others on my path.

I say Yes unconditionally to what is.

I open myself to every transformation that is ready to happen in
and through me.

I reclaim my body as a channel of spirituality; I celebrate my powers and passions.

I drop the need for certainty; I am comfortable with ambiguity.

I let go of fear and obligation and live by love and choice.

I keep finding an inner source of strength and comfort in and beyond me.

I disperse compassion and love wherever I go.

I consecrate myself to join with others to end war and injustice in my lifetime.

I keep finding new companions on my journey to love, wisdom, and healing.

I redeem the earth and include all humanity in my heart.

I look back over my life and all that has happened. I recall the people I have known and all they did to, with, or for me and all that I did to, with, or for them. I begin with my parents and end with the most recent person I have met. I see how it has been like a story; an order and continuity pervades it. I affirm a trust that it has a meaning. *Love makes meaning visible. I trust its power.*

I contemplate my lifeline with each of its turning points.

I notice the messages that limited or expanded me, for example, "Don't go," or "Don't go that far."

I see the afflicting and assisting forces, mortal and immortal, those who encouraged or repressed my lively energy.

I recall my griefs and how they were mourned, my gifts and how they were given.

Where was my effort and where was grace?

What were my breakthrough events of destiny and awakening?

Which crises and relationships were initiatory?

Which places or jobs opened me to new dimensions in myself?

Where were the opportunities to develop and release my gifts to the world?

How do I give thanks?

How did I befriend or deny my shadow, my dark, ego-inflated side as well as the bright, untapped potential in my Self?

If I believe that the way everything turns out after I have done all I can to fix or change things reveals my path, what is my path right now?

I picture this scene: all the characters on my life's stage take a bow. Villains and heroes become equal in this moment. All were necessary to the plot and the denouement. All were entertaining.

I greet each with compassion and thanks, realizing that this is what it took for me to become who I am.

My only search is for that which is always and already all of ours. Now what?

Epilogue

What follows is a version of a Hasidic story I once heard and that has stayed with me over the years. I find it so profound that I keep contemplating it, but I still do not feel that I have plumbed it fully. I share it in concluding this book because I believe it to be a wonderfully joyous account of the synchronicity of religious questions, spiritual consciousness, and the power of lively energy.

In the late 1800s, a young rabbi in a Polish farming village found himself at a loss to answer the unusually deep theological questions continually posed to him by his congregants. Though they were simple farmers and herders living in this *shtetl*, they were often ruminating on such questions as: Why is there suffering and evil in the world? Why does God not intervene to save the innocent? Why are there pogroms? What is the ultimate meaning of Passover? What happens after death? Not being a particularly sharp student at yeshiva/seminary, he had not emerged into rabbinical life with many answers. At times, he did not even quite understand the questions. The rabbi, however, did recall his best professor, a very ancient and eminently wise rabbi. One day, he wrote to him, asking if he would come to the *shul* some evening to answer all the puzzling questions for him. To his happy surprise, the great rabbi agreed.

A month later, all the congregation was abuzz with excitement that at last, their religious problems would be addressed and laid to rest. They were sitting in the candlelit synagogue in great awe and with ardent attentiveness as the sage from Krakow with his long white beard and stooped shoulders entered the sanctuary. The old man went up and stood silently before the *bima* (the lectern from which the Torah is read). After a contemplative moment, he sat quietly on a rude wooden chair facing the people. His voice was faint, but in the silence of expectation he could easily be heard: "I want to hear your questions, and then I will answer them—not one by one, but only after I have heard them all."

The congregants stood one at a time and asked their questions, wondering how the rabbi, who was certainly listening carefully, would be able to remember them all. After everyone who wanted to present his personal conundrum had done so, the wise old man peered out into the audience and asked if there was anyone else with a query. Only silence greeted him, the breathless silence of those who have waited a long time for satisfaction and were now about to find it. "Good," he murmured, "So now I will answer every single question." The little congregation was poised and arched toward their teacher, necks craned, ears pricked, eyes aglow with this assurance that their longtime enigmas would finally be cleared up.

The old rabbi looked back at them intently and with great kindliness. He began to hum a local *niggun,* a folk tune used in services to induce a prayerful attitude. The people stared at him and at one another. What could this mean? Was he humming as a prologue to his answering? Was he bored? But without explanation, their elder guide kept humming the tune they all knew so well.

After awhile, the people began to hum along in harmony with the rabbi. Some folks took out their fiddles or flutes and began to play softly to accompany the humming. Soon they were dancing and swaying as the evening became a party full of laughter and joy. The rabbi stayed in his seat smiling as he tapped his foot to the rhythm and continued humming.

Somewhat later, as people tired, they began to relax and grow quiet again. Now they looked to the rabbi quizzically. Would he now speak to their questions? And he did speak: "I have now fully answered all your questions," he announced, and bowing to them and to the Torah, he took his leave.

A *niggun* is a tune flowing in search of its own unattainable end.

—ABRAHAM JOSHUA HESCHEL

Such harmony is in immortal souls.

—WILLIAM SHAKESPEARE, *The Merchant of Venice*

About the Author

David Richo, Ph.D., M.F.T., is a psychotherapist, teacher, and writer in Santa Barbara and San Francisco, California, who emphasizes Jungian, transpersonal, and spiritual perspectives in his work. For more information, including a schedule of workshops and an audio catalogue, visit www.davericho.com.